S0-AGC-636

A Speechless Child
is the
Word of God

Dedicated
To My Beloved Father and Teacher
Edward Francis Mohler, Sr.
May He Rest in Peace

*S*aint Augustine
An Interpretation of

on The Trinity
Christ
Mary
Church
Authority
Sacraments
Prayer
Hope
and the Two Cities

A Speechless Child
is the
Word of God

James A. Mohler, S. J.

New City Press

Published in the United States by New City Press
86 Mayflower Avenue, New Rochelle, New York 10801
©1992 James A. Mohler, S.J.

Cover design by Nick Cianfarani

Library of Congress Cataloging-in-Publication Data:

Mohler, James A.
    A speechless child is the word of God : an interpretation of Saint
Augustine on the Trinity, Mary, church, authority, sacraments,
prayer, hope and the two cities / James A. Mohler.

    Includes bibliographical references and index.
    ISBN 0-56548-009-0 : $9.95
    1. Augustine, Saint, Bishop of Hippo.   I. Title.
BR65.A9M567   1992
230'.14'092—dc20   92-14867

Printed in the United States of America

TABLE OF CONTENTS

PROLOGUE

Augustine, fifth century bishop of Hippo, came at a crucial time in history with the fading of the Roman Empire and the height of the Christian Roman synthesis. With his rich background in the Roman classics and the popular Neoplatonic philosophy and his firm faith in Christ, he was able to integrate the best of both worlds—Christian and Roman.

Augustine helped formulate the great mysteries of Christianity such as the Trinity, Incarnation, the Virgin Mother of God, the Church and Sacraments into a language understandable to his parishioners, both the learned and the unschooled.

Although he was a great theologian, Augustine was also a kind pastor, preaching reconciliation with those who opposed the Church's teachings. Moreover, he spoke to his flock as a fellow sinner, never lording his episcopacy over them. Thus he is ever alongside them rather than ahead or over them on the road to salvation.

In the following essays we hope to examine Augustine's keen insights into the mysteries of God and his only Son who is embodied in his Church and sacraments. Also we will see the salient place of Christ's mother, the type and model of his Church, in Augustine's theology. Contemplation and prayer link Augustine to God, Father, Son and Holy Spirit, his threefold beacon of hope.

I.

THE TRINITY IS THE ONE, ONLY AND TRUE GOD

(*The Trinity* 1, 2)

Divine Triad

People have struggled long over the unity and diversity of God, allied to his transcendence and immanence. Sometimes this is confused with monotheism and polytheism. But in reality few peoples are polytheists in the sense that a number of gods are equal in power and wisdom.

More often the lesser gods are powers, personifications or hypostases of qualities of the main god, whether Brahman or Gitchee Manitou. Also lesser divinities are often links between the transcendent vanishing creator and his people. Moreover, the farther away God seems, the more the intermediaries tend to proliferate.

When we arrive at the Judaeo-Christian tradition, we see the development of many intermediaries like angels and hypostases like the divine Word (*dabar*), Wisdom (*hokmah*), Spirit (*ruah*) and King (*messiah*). Therein lies a problem. Are these hypostases lesser gods, creatures or what? Certainly the Hebrew tradition struggled to maintain its fundamental monotheism according to the Shema. Moreover, some have argued that various prophetic movements have fought to maintain monotheism against the growth of polytheism.

The Christian sect of Judaism arose in the rabbinic period in which there flourished a plethora of angels, intermediaries and hypostases. So Christianity had to wrestle with the same problem as contemporary rabbis, namely, how to preserve divine transcendence and yet maintain the popular network of intermediaries.

Some say that the angels and other messengers and hypostases were used to preserve divine transcendence and respect for the divine Name, so that God's Word, Wisdom or Spirit are substituted for the holy *Tetragrammaton* of the Hebrew Bible.

The Evolution of the Christian Doctrine of the Trinity

The Messiah, Son of God, Word of God and Holy Spirit are found in the Christian New Testament, as in contemporary Jewish literature. Christians, of course, identify Jesus of Nazareth with the expected Messiah. But some feel that it was only after the resurrection and pentecost experiences that his disciples recognized Jesus as the Messiah. And so they read this messianic message back into the pre-resurrection episodes such as the transfiguration and the temptations in the desert.[1]

Paul teaches his followers that the Father sent his Son and Holy Spirit (see Gal 4:4-7). Moreover, the Holy Spirit seems to be God's immanent presence in the souls of the just. Thus Paul gives us our earliest glimpses of the Christian Trinity. Moreover, he salutes the Corinthians (2 Cor 13:13), "The grace of our Lord, Jesus Christ, the love of God and the fellowship of the Holy Spirit be with you all." This seems to have been a common greeting or blessing in the early Christian community. Lex orandi est lex credendi. In other words, the people's faith is reflected in their prayers.[2]

Also Matthew gives us the early Christian baptismal formula (Mt 28:19). "In the name of the Father, Son and Holy Spirit." "In the name" signifies a liturgical dedication or consecration to God, Father, Son and Holy Spirit.

Hill[3] distinguishes between the economic and transcendental approach to the Trinity. While the former begins with the divine missions of the Son and Holy Spirit to mankind, the latter stresses the eternal mutual relationships of the divine hypostases—the mystery of the Trinity taken apart from creation. The economic approach includes the incarnation, salvation, sanctification, Church, sacraments, etc. The earliest Christians up to Nicaea favored the economic side of the Trinity.

While the Apostolic Fathers spread the gospel of Christ, the apologists were concerned with pagan polytheism.[4] Thus Justin (Apol) wrote that though Christians worship Christ in the second place and the Holy Spirit in the third, neither are adored separate from the Godhead of the Father. For both Word and Holy Spirit are God. Justin's school seems to teach a two-stage Logos, the first being an eternal and personal existence with the Father, while in the second the Logos is generated as Son by the will of the Father, but not eternally.[5] Draina feels (296) that the apologists are hesitant about the Holy Spirit and the unity and otherness of the Father and Son.

Irenaeus, writing against the Gnostics, calls the Son and the Holy Spirit

1. See E. Hill, The Mystery of the Trinity (London: Chapman, 1985), 36-38; henceforth Mystery.
2. See C. Draina, "The Holy Trinity in the Bible," New Catholic Encyclopedia, 14:306.
3. Hill, Mystery, 39-40.
4. See Draina, "The Holy Trinity," 14:296. This section depends on Draina (D).
5. See E. Fortman, The Triune God (Grand Rapids: Baker, 1982), 150.

the two hands of God, while, at the same time, defending the unity and trinity of the divinity. In Africa Tertullian (*Against Praxeas*) refutes monarchianism, while denying the eternal generation of the Son. He believes in the divinity of the Holy Spirit who proceeds from the Father through the Son. Tertullian, who influenced Nicaea, uses "person" and "trinity" of the Father, Son and Holy Spirit. Draina notes (296) that Tertullian shifts the focus

from the absolutely eternal moment to that in which the divine plurality becomes manifested in creation and redemption. The personalist idiom intensifies though not without presenting a difficulty.

Both Tertullian and Hippolytus saw the plurality of the salvific economy reaching back to the immanent life of the Godhead (297). But they defend the unity and trinity of God. Tertullian influenced the trinitarian doctrine of the Roman Church.

In Alexandria Origen teaches three hypostases in one God. Father and Son are of the same substance (*homoousios*). However, he leaves the door open to the subordination of the Son and Holy Spirit to the Father.

Nicaea I (325) against the Arians, declares the Son consubstantial (*homoousion*) with the Father, while Constantinople I (381) extends this to the Holy Spirit.

Draina (297) reminds us that heresies tend to oversimplify matters. Thus Arius, while defending the unique transcendence of the Father, concludes that the Son and the Holy Spirit must be high creatures. For the Father alone is eternal, all wise, good and uncommunicable.

Nicaea declares the divinity of Christ, while advancing the evolution of trinitarian doctrine. For the Son is begotten, not made, of the same substance as the Father, true God of true God, uncreated and eternal. However, some object that *homoousion* is a non-biblical concept, though it was to be affirmed by later councils. Moreover, Athanasius teaches that Father, Son and Holy Spirit are one in being but three separate hypostases. Hilary of Poitiers agrees.

But some such as Melitus of Antioch, Cyril of Jerusalem and Basil of Ancyra preferred *homoousion*, namely, that the Son is of like substance to the Father. Constantinople I (381) affirmed Nicaea, asserting the divinity of the Holy Spirit as well. One God with three hypostases or persons, Father, Son and Holy Spirit.

The Cappadocian Fathers meanwhile develop concepts of procession, property and relation in the Trinity, based on the New Testament. They stress the three hypostases and their properties, e.g., the ungenerateness of the Father and the generateness of the Son, while clarifying how the Godhead of the Father is communicated to the Son and Holy Spirit.

And whereas Gregory of Nyssa believes that the Holy Spirit proceeds from the Father through the Son, the West holds that the Holy Spirit proceeds from the Father and the Son (*filioque*) (*quicumque*) (D 301).

Victorinus and Ambrose

The Neoplatonist Victorinus, whose conversion inspired Augustine, helps lay the groundwork for Western trinitarian theology. For example, he believes that the Word is eternal and consubstantial with the Father. He also perceives a threefold power in God: being, living and understanding.[1] Moreover, the relationship of the Father and the Son is like that of the Platonic One and Nous, the Unknowable and the Knowable.

Opposing Arius, Victorinus opens the way for Augustine's psychological approach to the Trinity. For the human soul mirrors the triune Godhead in its existence, life and self-knowledge. If we are created in the image of God, we must reflect his threefold nature.

The Logos, the term of the Father's will, is his Son. Moreover, as his image he is also the term of the Father's understanding. In substance, power and dignity, the Son is equal to the Father. But as a person and Son he is less.

The Holy Spirit, who is from Christ, who, in turn, is from God, is consubstantial with the Father and Son. The three are mutually inexisting, three subsistences in one substance—being, life and intelligence.

Ambrose, Augustine's other mentor, while opposing the Arians, followed the Eastern view of the Trinity by considering the persons before the one divine nature. Though the Father is the principle of the Son and the Holy Spirit, they are coeternal with him. And the Son is not less than his Father as God, but only as human.

As Edmund Fortman remarks (138), Ambrose in his *On the Holy Spirit* wants to show that the Spirit is a divine person, coequal to and consubstantial with the Father and the Son. From the scriptures we see that the Holy Spirit is light, life, creator, Lord, eternal, gracious, forgiving, sanctifying and indwelling. The Spirit proceeds from the Father through the Son or from the Father and the Son. But the three inexist in each other, coeternal and coequal.

Augustine

As Portalié notes,[2] Augustine's theology of the Trinity perfects and passes on the traditions of the Church, harmonizing the divinity of the Son and the Holy Spirit with the unity of the Godhead. Whereas the Greeks and the Latins before him stressed the three persons in one nature, Augustine starts with the one divine nature subsisting in three persons. Some feel that although Augustine's approach avoids the dangers of tritheism and subordinationism, it could leave the door open to modalism. But, as Augustine reminds us often,

---

1. See Fortman, *The Triune God*, 135.
2. See E. Portalié, *A Guide to the Thought of St. Augustine* (Chicago: Regnery, 1960), 138; henceforth *Guide*.

he must speak of this ineffable mystery, even though in an imperfect manner due to the weakness of his wounded intellect.

The Greeks and Latins agree on the three persons who participate fully and equally in the one divine nature, one God, Trinity. So whatever is predicated to each person is, according to essence, predicated to all, but according to their relationship to each other.

Portalié[1] gives three characteristics of the Latin concept of the Trinity as it was influenced by Augustine. First, the theology of the Trinity starts with the one divine nature expressed in three persons. Second, all operations outside are attributed to the whole Trinity. Third, the psychological approach to the processions, with the human mind reflecting its triune divine image.

The early Christian view of the Trinity starts with the Father as the source of the divinity and also the source of the other two persons, so that the divinity seems to be especially his. However, Augustine starts with the one divine nature in which all three persons share equally and work together as a team. But the divine nature is appropriated to each person in a special way. Thus the Son became human and the Holy Spirit descended upon the apostles on Pentecost Sunday.

Clearly the Trinity is the cornerstone of Christian teaching as Augustine illustrates in his discourse to the bishops at the Council of Hippo (393). After speaking about the incarnation, Augustine remarks that belief is also required in the Holy Spirit, consubstantial and coeternal with the Father and Son. Three persons in one God, but not three gods. So one water is found in the spring, stream and drinking cup. And one tree has root, trunk and branch—all wood, but in three parts.

The relationship of the Father and the Son was discussed thoroughly by the Fathers—one nature and two persons, Begetter and Begotten, Principle and Image, though the Son differs in no respect and enjoys absolute equality with the Father.

The Holy Spirit, God's Gift, is less thoroughly explained. However, God does not communicate a gift less perfect than himself. So Augustine concludes that Father, Son and Holy Spirit are all God with the same substance.

The Trinity is an important part of Christian teaching (see *Christian Teaching*, chap. 9) (F), because the goal of our life is the enjoyment of the Father, Son and Holy Spirit. "The Trinity, one supreme Being, accessible to all who enjoy him," both Thing and Cause. "This Trinity is one God, from whom, through whom and in whom all things exist." Though the Father, Son and Holy Spirit, each is God, "at the same time they are all one God." For each "individually compromises the fullness of the divine substance," one substance. The Father is not the Son or the Holy Spirit, or vice versa, but all are eternal, immutable, majestic and powerful. "In the Father resides unity;

1. Portalié, *Guide*, 130.

in the Son equality; and in the Holy Spirit the perfect union of unity and equality."

On the Trinity

Augustine wrote his classical work on *The Trinity*,[1] beginning in his youth and finishing up his editing in his later years with many delays along the way (L 174). He is worried because some have circulated the early parts of his thesis before it was ready for publication. However, as he would be the first to admit, our search to fathom this august mystery is never finished until the final vision.

Augustine's main purpose in writing is pastoral rather than polemic, trying to make sense of this fundamental truth for his Hippo flock. For background he read thoroughly the Latin sources. While books 1-7 study scriptures and the Fathers while answering objections, books 8-15 seek trinitarian analogies in human nature. In the first part Augustine notes that scriptures do not show any subordination of the Son and Holy Spirit to the Father, despite the fact that they are "begotten" and "sent." Furthermore, Old Testament apparitions of God are really angels.

People tend to think of God corporally, spiritually or to believe false things about him (1, 1). Scripture uses creature analogies for the Creator, "adapting itself to the little ones," so they can rise up to divine things, and also in order to "arouse the affections of the weak." Only rarely does scripture say things proper to God, such as "I am who am" (Ex 3:14).

It is hard to see how God can make changeable things, and yet he is not changeable himself. Since our sight is dimmed because of our sinfulness, it needs to be purified and healed in order to see "that ineffable thing in an ineffable manner."

Why are the Father, Son and Holy Spirit called persons (7, 4)? "Because that which is a person is common to them." The Greeks used the term "substance." Thus three substances and one essence. But Augustine prefers three persons and one essence or substance. We need to use these terms to guard against misinterpretations. Augustine fears the use of three essences lest diversity be placed in the unity of the divinity. However, there must be three somethings, persons or substances, but one essence. He prefers the essence of God to his substance and three persons rather than three substances in the Trinity.

In God "to be" and "to be a person" are the same. But in relation to each other the person of the Father equals the substance of the Father or the Father

---

1. Unless otherwise noted, quotes in this section are from *The Trinity* (398-420, 425) (F).

himself. Why do we call them three persons? In answer to the question: three what? Certainly not three animals or three human beings.

The Father is not the Son or the Holy Spirit and whatever is said of each in relationship to each other, for example, Word or Gift. "It is for this reason that the plural number is permitted." "I and the Father are one" (Jn 10:30). "We" and "us" are used of God in the Bible (see Gn 1:26; Jn 14:23). Mankind is made in the image and likeness of God, "in our image." In order that we might subsist in the trinitarian model of God.

Though we approach God through our likeness, we are drawn away by our unlikeness to him. Obviously we are not the Trinity, but only weak images. While the Son is a perfect reflection of his Father, we are defective resemblances of God.

The three persons are to be understood so that no member of the Trinity is less than another. "Hence there may be neither a confusion of persons, nor such a distinction whereby there would be some inequality." If we cannot reason to this, we should take it on faith. As Isaiah says (7:9): believe in order to understand.

In his preface to book 8, Augustine comments:

> Those names which are predicated relatively, the one of the other, are properly spoken of as belonging to each person in particular as the Father, Son and Holy Spirit, who is the Gift of both.

When spoken of singularly, the three persons are referred to the one, Trinity. For example, the Father is God, good, omnipotent, etc. So there are not three gods, goods or omnipotences. For the three persons *to be* is *to be great, wise, good,* etc.

No person is greater than another, nor less than the Trinity itself. Moreover, the Trinity itself is just as great as each person and just as true (8, 1). Each in each, all in each, each in all, all in all, all—one (6, 10).

The Father and Son together are one essence, one greatness, one truth, one wisdom; but not one Word or one Son, both of which express relationship. Wisdom, on the contrary, equals essence and so Father and Son are one Wisdom.

Though the Father does not equal the Son, vis-a-vis their mutual relationship, "They do not on that account cease to be one essence, since the relationship between them is only made known by these names." However, both together are one wisdom and one essence.

Christ is the power and wisdom of God, yet his power and wisdom are from the Father, who is power and wisdom (7, 3). Christ is the light and source of life from the Father, as well.

Father and Son both are one light, one God and one wisdom, "But the Son has been made for us the wisdom of God and justice and sanctification" because we turn to him in time in order to be with him eternally. The Son is the image of the Father. And so are we. However, we are not equal to the Son, since we are made by the Father through the Son.

Holy Spirit

The Holy Spirit is not only the love joining the Father and Son, but also is wisdom and light. So Father, Son, Holy Spirit—one light, one wisdom and one essence. "In the Trinity, 'to be' is nothing else than 'to be God,' and, therefore, there is one God, Father, Son and Holy Spirit."

So the Holy Spirit is true God (1, 6). "The Holy Spirit is certainly equal to the Father and Son and is consubstantial and coeternal with them in the unity of the Trinity." Thus we worship (*latreuein*) the Spirit.

Moreover, our bodies are both members of Christ and temples of the Holy Spirit (see 1 Cor 6:19, 15, 20). And though Christ sends the Spirit from the Father (see Jn 15:26), the Advocate is not to be considered less than the Father and Son. Both the Father and the Holy Spirit glorify the Son. And the Holy Spirit is received from the Father and the Son. So when the Spirit glorifies the Son, the Father also glorifies the Son. But "they are equal who mutually glorify each other" (2, 4).

Moreover, as the Son was sent in visible form, so the Holy Spirit came as a dove, wind and tongues of fire (2, 5). The Spirit is invisible and unchangeable like the Father and Son.

In the sense that the hearts of men, being moved by these external signs, might be turned away from the temporal manifestations of his coming to the hidden eternity of him who is forever present.

However, we cannot call the Spirit both God and dove as Jesus Christ is both God and man. Furthermore the dove and tongues may well have been seen in a spiritual vision.

The Father begot, while the Son was begotten; the Father sent, while the Son was sent. However, Father and Son are one. "And the Holy Spirit is one with them because these three are one." Whereas the Son was born and sent from the Father, the Holy Spirit is a gift of God (4, 20), proceeding from the Father and the Son. For "the one and the same Spirit is called the Spirit of the Father and the Son." Thus Jesus Christ breathed on the apostles, giving them the Holy Spirit (see Jn 20:22), a symbol that the Spirit proceeds from both the Father and the Son. "The Spirit of God is one, the Spirit of the Father and the Son, the Spirit who works all things in all" (1 Cor 12:6). The Holy Spirit was given twice. "The Father will send in my name" (Jn 14:26). "The Father is the principle of the whole divinity—of the whole Godhead" (4, 20). He who proceeds from the Father and the Son is referred back to him from whom the Son was born.

Although the Spirit had spoken through the prophets and inspired Zachary, Mary and John the Baptist, he was not given to the Church until Jesus was glorified (see Jn 7:39). Moreover, this theophany was unique with the gift of tongues, signifying the universality of the Church.

The Father, Son and Holy Spirit are one and the same substance, God the Creator, the omnipotent Trinity, who work together inseparably. Moreover, this great mystery cannot be represented adequately by a creature or by human words. For example, "the whole Trinity produced the flesh of the Son and the dove of the Holy Spirit, although each is referred to as a particular person."

> Things in the same Trinity that are properly predicated of each person are by no means predicated of them as they are in themselves, but in their relation either to one another or to the creature. It is obvious that such things are predicated of them relatively, and not in regard to their substance. (5, 11)

So the Trinity is God, great, good, eternal and omnipotent. However, we cannot say that the Trinity is the Father except metaphorically, for example, in his relationship to his adopted sons and daughters, who are regenerated through grace.

Furthermore, although the Trinity cannot be called the Son, it can be named the Holy Spirit in the universal sense that God is Spirit. However, if the name Spirit is applied to the third person of the Trinity, it denotes relation. For the Holy Spirit is the Spirit of the Father and the Son, the Gift of God.

The Holy Spirit is the ineffable communion of the Father and the Son. The Father and Son are both spirit and holy; and the Advocate is the gift of both.

The Spirit is the love and sweetness of the Begetter and the Begotten, going out to all according to their capacity (6, 10).

Augustine spends much time in his final book on the Trinity in discussion of the Holy Spirit. "We shall speak about the Holy Spirit, insofar as God, the Giver, shall permit." This Spirit of the Father and the Son is "the common love by which the Father and Son mutually love each other" (15, 17).

Scripture tells us that God is love (see 1 Jn 4:16). Why? "Because love itself is a substance worthy of the name of God." And just as the Word is called wisdom, even though the Father and Spirit also are wisdom, what is more fitting than to call God's gift—love? So the Spirit is called love, even though in the universal sense, the Father and Son also are love. God's Gift causes us to remain in him and him in us. "But love does this, so the Holy Spirit is the God who is Love." The Holy Spirit inflames us with love for God and our neighbor. For we do not have the means to love God on our own. John says that we should love God because he loved us first (see 1 Jn 4:7-19). Paul adds: "The love of God is poured forth in our hearts by the Holy Spirit" (Rom 5:5) (15, 17).

Although other gifts are given by the Spirit, love is the most important, enabling us to love God and neighbor. "Love, then, which is from God and is God, is properly the Holy Spirit, through whom the charity of God is poured forth in our hearts, through whom the Trinity dwells in us" (15, 18). Love, then, is God's greatest gift. "What more logical than that he himself should be love, who is called both God and of God? And what is more proper than the Spirit common to the Father and the Son should properly be called Love?

Hill[1] sums up Augustine's theology of the Holy Spirit. First of all, the Holy Spirit proceeds from the Father and the Son, as the New Testament teaches us. Second, the Holy Spirit is the common fellowship, comradeship and love of the Father and the Son. Third, the Holy Spirit proceeds from the Father and the Son, as from one origin or principle and proceeds from the Father principally, who is the origin of origins. Finally, the Father's monarchy, *primus inter pares*, is preserved.

Analogies

Whereas in books 1-4 of his *The Trinity* Augustine establishes belief in the Trinity from scriptures and in his opposition to the Arians (books 5-7), in books 8-10 he takes the interior path to the divine mystery. We can know the Trinity imperfectly in the mirror of our own mind or soul, since the Bible tells us that we are made in the image and likeness of God. An important triple analogy is that of the lover, beloved and love (book 8).

Also when the mind knows and loves itself, "a trinity remains: mind, love and knowledge." And although each is a substance in itself, there is no confusion. For "all are found mutually in all" (9, 5). The mind, knowledge and love are inseparable, yet each is its own substance and all together constitute one substance or essence. And their names signify their mutual relationships.

Memory, understanding and will constitute another triad that reflects the Trinity (10, 11). Our memory, understanding and will are one life, one mind and one substance. Moreover, they are called memory, understanding and will in relation to something else. "Yet each in respect to itself is life, mind and essence." So the three are one. "They are three in that they are mutually referred to each other." If not equal, they certainly would not comprehend each other. "Each is comprehended by each one. But all are also comprehended by each one." Thus I can remember my understanding and will.

Our external trinity in our sensitive life consists of: the object seen, our outer vision and the attention of our mind (11, 2). It is evil if according to this outer trinity which is concerned with sensible and corporeal things we

---

1. Hill, *Mystery*, 111.

use our imagination to beget another trinity: memory, interior vision and will. For the outer triad is not an image of God, "since it is produced in the soul through the senses of the body." However, it is not totally dissimilar because all created things are good and so reflect divine goodness, though these can be defective images.

"An image is only an expression of God in the full sense, when no other nature lies between it and God." "The vision which takes place in the sense is mingled with something spiritual." Moreover, the will, conforming vision with bodily form, suggests the Holy Spirit (11, 2).

Augustine prefers the interior threesome: memory, inner vision and will (11, 3), when these are drawn together (*coguntur*) and are called thought (*cogitatio*).

An even better triad is the inner memory of the mind, remembering itself, the inner understanding by which it understands itself and the inner will by which it loves itself. And these three are always together (14, 7).

But the epitome of Augustine's inner trinity does not consist of the mind remembering, understanding and loving itself, "but because it can also remember, understand and love him by whom it was made," and in whose image it was made. And when it does this, the mind becomes wise. "Let it, then, remember God, to whose image it has been made, understand him and love him" (14, 12). Moreover, when the mind worships its Creator, it is capable of him and can partake of him.

In his final book, which we will see more of later, Augustine notes that it is in love, which God is called in scripture, that "the Trinity began to dawn a little," that is, the lover, beloved and love, which triad he had discussed in book 8 (15, 6).

Though we wish to raise ourselves up to the Trinity, we are unable. We see trinities outside and inside of us, as our mind is known and thinks of itself. Does the mind know of itself or "when it beholds something eternal and unchangeable which itself is not"?

Do we see trinities because they are either wrought within us or are in us when we remember, behold and will them, "so in some such way we also see the Trinity, that is God, because there by our understanding we also behold him, as it were speaking his Word, that is, the Father and Son and the Love proceeding from them and common to both, namely, the Holy Spirit"?

Or do we see rather than believe these trinities pertaining to our senses and mind, but we believe rather than see that God is the Trinity (15, 6)?

Wisdom, God, knows and loves himself. "There is a trinity, that is, wisdom, the knowledge of itself and the love of itself. For so we find a trinity in us, i.e., the mind, the knowledge, by which it knows itself and the love by which it loves itself." Though mind, knowledge and love are in us, they are not equal to our person or our soul. But "that Trinity of which our mind is an image, is nothing else in its totality than the triune God." Though the three divine persons are one essence, they are not the same as each human individual is one person.

Book 15

This final book of Augustine's *The Trinity* gives us a good summary of his thought on the subject. Why should we puzzle over such a deep mystery? So that we might know our Creator through his created image, "if we are able" (15, 1). Is not this a hopeless task, since the Trinity is incomprehensible here below? Faith seeks, while understanding finds, moving from the visible to the invisible (see Rom 1:20). So Augustine starts with creation and proceeds through certain trinities until he arrives at the human mind, as we have seen.

"The Trinity, of which the mind is an image, is nothing else in its totality than God, nothing else in its totality than the Trinity" (15, 7). Three persons in one God, one essence, but not as an individual man or woman is one person. Three, therefore, memory, understanding and love (or will), in that unchangeable essence which is God.

But we still see the Trinity only dimly as in a mirror (15, 8). We have, therefore, tried to do this in order that through this image, which we are, we might see him by whom we have been made, in some manner or other as through a mirror (see 1 Cor 13:12; 2 Cor 8:18).

There is a great enigma, Augustine notes (15, 9) "that we do not see what is impossible for us not to see."

Our external word is a sign of our internal word. "So the Word of God was made flesh by assuring that in which it may be manifested to the senses of men and women" (15, 11). "By assuming it, not by being consumed in it this word of ours becomes a sound and that Word became flesh."

There can be no work unless a word precedes it. "Just as the Word of God could be, even though no creature existed. But no creature could be except through that Word, through whom all things were made." Thus the Trinity did not become flesh, though the whole Trinity brought the incarnation about so that we could follow Christ's example.

The Word, therefore, the only begotten Son of God, the Father, like and equal in all things to the Father, God of God, Light of Light, Wisdom of Wisdom, Essence of Essence. He is wholly the same as the Father, because this is the Son and that is the Father.
Moreover, he would not have uttered himself completely and perfectly, if there were anything less or more in his Word than in himself. (15, 14)

For the Son can do nothing of himself. "But only what he sees his Father doing" (Jn 5:15).

The Father, therefore, "knows all things in himself and he knows all things in his Son, but in himself, as himself, and in the Son as his Word which is spoken concerning all those things which are in himself." "Father and Son, therefore, know each other mutually, but the former by begetting and the latter by being born." "God alone may be understood to have an eternal Word coeternal with himself" (15, 15).

So far in book 15 Augustine has been speaking of the Father and the Son. Now he talks of the Holy Spirit.

Insofar as we have been able to see through this mirror and this enigma, now we are able to speak about the Holy Spirit, insofar as God, the Giver, shall permit it. (15, 17)

Here again, Augustine underlines the mystery of the Trinity. For due to our own sinfulness we can see only a dim reflection of the Trinity within ourselves. Yet we do see something and hope for a full vision in heaven.

The Holy Spirit is the Spirit of the Father and the Son. "He insinuates to us the common love by which the Father and Son mutually love each other." For God is love (see 1 Jn 4:16).

However, the memory is not in one person, the Father, while the understanding is in the Son and love only in the Holy Spirit. Moreover, if the Father, Son and Holy Spirit are wisdom, so all together may be called Love.

"Yet it is not without reason that in this Trinity only the Son is called the Word of God and that only the Holy Spirit is the Gift of God. And that only he, of whom the Son was begotten and from whom the Holy Spirit principally proceeds is God the Father."

Since the Father begot the Son, "the common Gift should also proceed from the Son and the Holy Spirit should be the Spirit of both." "If, then, any one of these three is to be specially called Love, what more fitting than that this should be the Holy Spirit."

The First Letter of John tells us that God is love. "We know that we abide in him and he in us because he has given us his Spirit." "Therefore, the Holy Spirit, whom he has given us causes us to remain in God and God in us. But love does this. He is, therefore, the God who is love."

The Holy Spirit proceeds from God, his Gift to us, inflaming us with love for God and neighbor. For the Holy Spirit is love. We love God because he loved us first (see 1 Jn 4:7-19). The charity of God is poured into our hearts by the Holy Spirit who has been given to us (see Rom 5:5).

"The Holy Spirit is especially called the Gift for no other reason except love." However, the whole Trinity dwells in us, and not just the Holy Spirit (15, 18). Though he is God's Gift to us, the Holy Spirit is himself God and without any subordination of Gift to Givers. But rather "the concord between the Gift and the Givers" (15, 19).

If the Love whereby the Father loves the Son, and the Son the Father, reveals in an ineffable manner the union between both, what more fitting than that he, who is the Spirit, common to both, should be properly called love?

Moreover, for Augustine the will is the faculty of love. "If the will of God is also to be specially attributed to any one person in the Trinity, then this name, just as love, belongs more appropriately to the Holy Spirit. For what else is love than will?" (15, 20). Augustine tries

> to make God the Father and God the Son known to us, that is, God, the begetter, who in some way has uttered everything that he has in his substance in his Word, coeternal with himself, and his Word, God himself, who likewise has nothing more nor less than what was in him, who truly begot his Word so we could see him enigmatically (see 1 Cor 13:12) in our own mind with its threefold faculties.

The birth of the Son from the Father is apart from time, as is the procession of the Holy Spirit (15, 26).

> Just as the Father has in himself that the Holy Spirit should proceed from him so that he has given to the Son that the same Holy Spirit should proceed from him and both apart from time. And that when the Holy Spirit is said to proceed from the Father, it is to be understood that his proceeding also from the Son comes to the Son from the Father. For if whatever he has, the Son has from the Father, then certainly he has from the Father that the Holy Spirit also proceeds from him. (15, 26)

While the Son is born of the Father, "the Holy Spirit proceeds principally from the Father, and since the Father gives without any interval of time, he proceeds from both in common." So the Son has from the Father that the Holy Spirit also proceeds from him. And so the Holy Spirit has from the Father that he also proceeds from the Son just as from the Father (15, 27).

Augustine now relates a sermon which he had given to his flock explaining the opaqueness of this great mystery (15, 27). Let them use prayer, study and morality in their search for understanding, "that what is retained by faith may be seen in the mind," insofar as it can. Moreover, they should not deny the mystery just because they cannot see it. As far as Augustine is concerned, "I have said nothing worthy of the ineffability of that highest Trinity."

Taking the advice he had given to his people, Augustine feels that it is better to close his book on the Trinity with a prayer, rather than going on with further discussion and speculation (15, 28).

"O Lord, our God, we believe in you, Father, Son and Holy Spirit." Truth has revealed baptism in the name of the Trinity and the one God of the Shema. Seeking to understand what he believes, Augustine continues his prayer. "I have argued and labored much." Confessing his strength and weakness, his knowledge and ignorance, he asks the Lord to receive him and open up the closed doors of his mind.

"May I remember you, understand you and love you. Increase these gifts in me until you have reformed me completely." Furthermore, he asks deliverance from his own distracting words and thoughts. For while words fall short, "You, as One, shall remain." For all that Augustine has written comes from one God, Trinity. "If anything comes from myself, may you and yours forgive me, Amen."

On John: The Trinity is One God

In his *Commentary on John* (20, 3) (N) Augustine notes that the Father and Son are inseparable, God and Word, "bound together by charity, one God, and the Spirit of charity also one. So Father, Son and Holy Spirit are the Trinity." Thus we have also the inseparability of the divine persons and their works. Though the Father, Son and Holy Spirit are one God, they are not three gods (29, 2). The Father is not the Son and vice versa, nor is he the Holy Spirit, nor also is the Son the Holy Spirit or is the Spirit either the Father or the Son, but rather one God.

The Trinity is one God, one eternity, one majesty, triune, but not three gods. "The Father is God as respects himself, but he is Father as respects his Son. And the Son is God as respects himself, although he is Son as regards his Father." Thus Father and Son are names given relatively. So also a human father is a man in himself, but a father in relationship to his Son.

If the Father, Son and Holy Spirit are three, what three are they? Augustine replies, "If you ask: 'three what?' number ceases." Certainly they are not three almighties or three creators. "Only in relation to each other do they suggest number, not in their essential existence."

On Pentecost there were many hearts becoming one heart. This is even more true in God, the very fountain of love in the Father and Son. As the Holy Spirit is the principle of loving unity in the Church, so also in the Trinity.

> If then the love of God is shed abroad in our hearts by the Holy Spirit, which is given to us, makes many souls one soul and many hearts one heart, how much rather are Father, Son and Holy Spirit one God, one life, one beginning. (5)

Letter to Maximus: Coeternal Wisdom[1]

Latreia (divine worship) is owed to the holy Trinity, Father, Son and Holy Spirit. Yet the Father is not the Son, nor is the Holy Spirit the Father and Son. "Since in that Trinity the Father is the Father of the Son alone and the Son is

---

1. Letter 170 to Maximus, physician and convert from Arianism.

the Son of the Father alone, but the Holy Spirit is the Spirit of the Father and the Son."

The Son is not a creature, rather "the Father begot the Son of his own substance." Moreover, he was not begotten in time, so the Father has never been without the Son.

Wisdom is coeternal with the light whose brightness it is, God, the Father. Nor is the Holy Spirit a creature, but rather proceeds eternally from the Father and the Son.

The Trinity is of one and the same nature and substance, not less in each person than in all, or more in all than in each; and as much in the Father alone or in the Son alone as in the Father and Son together; and as much in the Holy Spirit alone as in the Father, Son and Holy Spirit together.

The Father did not become less when he begot his Son. "He begot him as another self so as to remain whole in himself and to be as great in the Son as he is alone."

Furthermore, the Holy Spirit is a whole person from a whole person. The Spirit is both with him and from him. Moreover, the Spirit does not diminish him by proceeding from him or increase him by remaining with him.

"All three persons are not confused by the one or separated by the three. But rather because they are one, they are three, and because they are three they are one." If he can make the many hearts of the faithful one heart (Acts 4:32), why cannot he make the three persons one God, to whom we owe *latreia*?

The terms Father, Son and Holy Spirit do not denote the divine nature, but rather the Person of each toward the other, implying analogy and relationship. Though the Father and Son each is God, one is not more God than the other. In origin the Father is God, from whom the Son is God.

The Father begot his Son eternally "with such complete equality to himself that the Son does not excel him either in power or in age." The Son attributes all he has to his Father from whom he received equality. And since he is always born, he is always equal.

However, is not the Father greater, since the Son became man, taking on the form of a servant, less than the Trinity and the angels (see Heb 2:9) and less than his own parents? The Son became man, while, at the same time, remaining God. Though Christ, as human, is less than his Father, as God he is equal to the Father and equally God.

The Psychology of the Trinity

Through his psychological approach to the Trinity, Augustine has given us some good insights into the person and personality of both God and man. He made use of Aristotle's fourth category of relation. Thus the Son can be related to the Father, and at the same time be the same substance, because relation transcends substance.[1]

In the Post-Niceaen era the concept of person was developed in order to try to explain the trinitarian definitions of the council. Previous attempts had used the analogy of the world proceeding from God, leading to a type of subordinationism. But Augustine used man, mind and soul in lieu of the universe and cosmos as an analogy of the inner life of God and the divine processions, perhaps reflecting the interiority of Neoplatonism.

We have seen some of Augustine's psychological triads, reflecting our triune Maker. For example: existence, knowledge and love of both; being, knowing and willing; being, having form and following law; love, beloved and love; object seen, external vision and will; being, understanding and life; mind, knowledge and love; memory, understanding and will; ability, learning and use; and, finally, our memory, understanding and love of God.[2]

We can be persons only insofar as we are related to our Creator, Father, Son and Holy Spirit, in whose image we are made and whose eternal and temporal image is the Son of God made man, remembering, understanding and loving our Maker.

Personality is to relation as history is to creation. So our personality is our individual history beginning with our relationship with our Creator. For although a person may be absolute *in se*, he or she is essentially *ad alium*, that is, related to others.

For example, the person of the Son consists of his relationship of sonship and begottenness. And our human personality is constituted in its relationship to our parents and God. Henry comments, "In both the human image and the divine prototype, personality expresses itself in relation, communicability, sharing, togetherness, etc."[3]

Jesus Christ is the paradigm of the personal. For all he has is from the Father and in his human nature he is related to all men and women and to all creatures who are also images of the Father. While the Father begets his Son, the Holy Spirit proceeds from the Father and the Son as from a single principle. However, the Greeks preferred to say that the Advocate proceeds from the Father through the Son.

Conclusion

As we have seen, Augustine starts out his discussions of the Trinity with the one divine nature, thereby eliminating dangers of subordinationism and

1. See P. Henry, *St. Augustine on Personality* (New York: Macmillan, 1960); henceforth *On Personality*.
2. See Portalié, *Guide*, 134-35; *The City of God* 11, 27; *Confessions* 13, 11; *The Trinity* 8, 10; 11, 2; 11, 3; 6, 10; 10, 11; 14, 12; 14, 2.
3. Henry, *On Personality*, 137.

tritheism, yet, perhaps, opening the door a bit for modalism. The three persons share in the same divine essence and operations, though certain actions such as the incarnation and sanctification are appropriated to the Son and Holy Spirit respectively.

The three persons are subjects of one divine activity, although relationally distinct, "three relationally distinct subsistences in one intellectual divine nature."[1]

The Holy Spirit is the gift and love, proceeding from the Father and Son as from one principle. The whole Trinity indwells and sanctifies the newly baptized soul, though this is appropriated to the Spirit.

Augustine gives us many natural and human triads which reflect our triune Creator. However, we most resemble our Maker when we remember, understand and love him.

Augustine is a vital link between the past trinitarian traditions of the New Testament and the Fathers and the future medieval theologians. His contributions include: his harmonizing of the divinity of the Son and Holy Spirit with the unity of God; his beginning with the one divine nature in which the three persons participate; his belief that all divine operations *ad extra* should be attributed to the whole Trinity, though they can have a special relationship to one person; his psychological analogies to the processions of the divine persons.

In the following chapter we will discuss more in detail the Son, the second person of the holy Trinity, who became man for our salvation and who was a special inspiration to Augustine in his conversion and later life.

---

1. Fortman, *The Triune God*, 142.

II.

HE IS BOTH A SPEECHLESS CHILD
AND HE IS THE WORD

(Sermon 189)

The God-Man

Having seen something of the development of the theology of the Trinity in Augustine's thought, let us now contemplate the divine Word, God's Son, who became human in order to redeem the world and to live on in his Church.

When Jesus lived in Galilee, some saw him as an itinerant rabbi or maggid; others, a Messiah; some, the Son of God, etc. Some felt that his messiahship died with him on the cross, while others believed that he had risen from the dead to reign in heaven.

Jesus' messiahship cannot be separated from his kingdom. However, he is not a military leader, but rather a spiritual one. While Yahweh is the true king of Israel, the Messiah is his vice regent, reigning over the whole world. At the time of Jesus there was high expectation of the imminent coming of the kingdom. The realm of God is both now and then; now in anticipation and then in the millennium of peace. However, most Jews hoped for a temporal reign, rather than a spiritual one.

John identifies Jesus with God's Memra or Logos. The Father's Word and his are one, for he and the Father are one. Moreover, he is God's creative Word (see Jn 1:1-14), echoing Philo. The Word became flesh and dwelt among us (1:14). Not only does Jesus teach the word of the Father, he is it (1:18). For he is both in the bosom of the Father and makes him known.

Is Jesus the Son of God? And if so, how does he differ from other Israelite sons and daughters of God? Did Jesus claim to be the Son of God in the sense that he is equal to the Father, which would have been considered blasphemy at the time, or was this relationship something which later Christians saw in retrospect? In other words, did God become man, or did man become God?

For the Jews of Jesus' era, the Father is God alone according to the Shema, though some began to see certain manifestations of Yahweh such as his Memra and Shekhinah as divine.

In the Hebrew tradition the title Son of God, was given to leaders, angels and kings of Israel (see Ps 2). Roman emperors also claimed the honor.

26

Moreover, the Qumran monks called the Messiah begotten of Adonai (*Rule Annex* 2, 11).

The infancy narratives of Jesus confirm his divine origins (see Lk 1:35); and other New Testament passages as well (see Mt 16:16, 26:63; Jn 20:31). The school of John leaves little doubt about Jesus' divine sonship (see Jn 3:16-18). The Father sent his Son to save the world through belief in him. And those who believe will share in his sonship (see Jn 1:12, 20:3, 20:17).

The incarnation of the Son of God is a deep mystery, leading to different interpretations in the early Church, some seeing Jesus as a holy man or prophet, while others claim he is wholly divine with only a semblance of humanity. In the early *kerygma* (Acts 2:36) God raises up the man Jesus. Apocryphal literature describes a preexisting Messiah. But if Jesus preexisted with the Father, how can we explain his humanity? Paul speaks of a divine emptying in order to take on human form (see Phil 2:5-11). Various views from adoptionism to docetism evolved.

While Jesus' divinity is well hidden in Mark, it is more evident in Matthew and Luke. And by the time of John's writing, the divinity and preexistence of the Messiah is fully seen.[1]

While the Gnostics and the Docetists feel that there is little need for humanity in Christ, Paul notes that God became man to save us from our sins. The Letter to the Hebrews shows the human side of Christ, who suffered and was tempted. He is the new high priest and mediator between God and us. Moreover, he is a perfect priest because he is without sin.

The early Church split into schools of interpretation of the incarnation from Adoptionists and Gnostics to Arians and Nestorians. Moreover, as Christianity became hellenized, there were new attempts at speculating and philosophizing over the God-Man, the preexisting Logos of God. The early Church's memory of the risen Christ mixes human and divine, Lord and Christ, our Lord and brother.

Does the preexisting Logos preclude the humanity of Jesus? Some early Christians called him the Son of Man, a high angel, the Son of God, Logos, Wisdom, etc. Theologians and Church councils tried to clarify the matter. For example, Nicaea (325) taught the consubstantiality of the Word with the Father against the Arians, while Ephesus (431), opposing the Nestorians, said that there is only one person in Christ; and the Council of Chalcedon (451), arguing against Eutyches, asserted the two distinct natures in Christ, divine and human.

---

1. See J. Knox, *The Humanity and Divinity of Christ* (Cambridge, 1967), 25.

Augustine Converted to Christ

When Augustine was converted and baptized by Ambrose (387), he was drawn to Christ who would be his savior and guide for the rest of his life. Still struggling with his weak flesh and his doubting mind, he feels that his great joy will be when he embraces the mediator between God and man, "the man Christ Jesus, who is over all things, God blessed forever, and who is the way, truth and the life" (Rom 9:5, Jn 14:6). The Word was made flesh so that Wisdom who made all might give us infants nourishing milk.

In the beginning, Augustine recalls in his *Confessions* (7, 18),[1] "I did not hold fast to Jesus, my God, a humble man, clinging to him who was humble. Nor did I know in what thing his lowliness would be my teacher." God's Word, eternal Truth, raises up the lowly. For he had built for himself a home of our clay, where he heals us in his weakness.

However, the young Augustine had some doubts about the divinity of Christ, rather seeing him as a great teacher (7, 19). The great mystery of the Word made flesh seemed inconceivable to him. As he read about Jesus' life in the gospels, he notes, "I had learned only that flesh did not cleave to your Word except together with a human soul and mind."

Anyone who knows the immutability of God's word, knows this. Augustine understood it as far as he could. For since scripture is true, "I acknowledge that in Christ was a complete man," not just a mindless body, but a "true man." Christ was a man above all human beings because of his superior human nature and wisdom, but as yet not God.

Later Augustine learned of the Word made flesh, a Catholic truth opposing Photinus who claimed that Christ was only a divinely inspired man. After his conversion, Augustine prayed to Christ Jesus, his helper and redeemer, who cast from him his follies, pleasures and lusts.

He writes of Jesus Christ, the true mediator, for we cannot convert ourselves. Some seek out false mediators such as Satan. But the true mediator is immortal and sinless. He "must be something like God and something like us." The true mediator is humble, showing himself to the humble. "Christ Jesus appeared between mortal sinners and the immortal just one." "Christ is mortal like human beings and just like God" (10, 43).

"As man, Christ is mediator; but as Word, he is in no middle place, since he is equal to God, with God and together one God." The Father so loved us that he gave his only Son for us sinners. "Equal to you, he became obedient to the death on the cross." He had the power to lay down his life and take it up again. So for us he is both victim and victor and "victor for the reason that he is victim."

Moreover, he is both priest and sacrifice, and "priest because he is the sacrifice." He makes us sons and daughters in lieu of servants since being

---

1. Quotes in this section are from the *Confessions*.

born of God, he became a servant for us. He will heal all our diseases. And while sitting at the right hand of his Father, he makes intercession for us. One would think that God's Word is far away and so fall into despair unless he had been made flesh and dwelt among us (see Jn 1:14). Though Augustine fears his many sins, he remembers that Christ died for all that all may live in him who died for them (see 2 Cor 5:15). Therefore, he casts his cares on the Lord to live that the Lord may teach and heal him. For his Son redeemed him with his blood.

Augustine beseeches God through his Son, our Lord, Jesus Christ sitting at his right hand. "As your mediator and ours, through whom you have sought us when we did not seek you, and sought us that we might seek you . . . Your Word through whom all things were made and called believers to adoption" (11, 2).

Faith, Creed and Works

Augustine spoke of the incarnation to the assembled bishops at Hippo (*Faith and Creed,* 3) (393) (F). "We believe in Jesus Christ, the Son of God, the only begotten of the Father, one God, our Lord." The Word of God is nothing like our words which vanish as soon as they are spoken. No, God's Word abides in a changeless state (see Jn 14:6). The Son is called the Word of the Father "because it is through him that the Father is made known. . . . Wisdom, which the Father begot, is most fittingly styled his Word. Since it is through him that the innermost nature of the Father is revealed to worthy souls." "In begetting the Word, God begot the same nature as himself." So the Word is not created.

The Father wanted to reveal himself, "begetting that selfsame reality which is one with him who has begotten it." The Son is called the Power and Wisdom of the Father because the Father made and ordered all things through him.

The Son is not made by the Father or begotten in time (4). For "the eternally wise God enjoys the eternal possession of his Wisdom." Although the Son is equal to his Father, he is not the same person as his Father. Nor is the Son a creature, for he is the Creator of all things. Yet God's Word did become a creature, humbling himself to show us the way to God (see Phil 2:6, 7).

Though the "Only Begotten" has no brothers or sisters, the "First Born" calls all those brothers and sisters who are "born again unto God's grace through filial adoption" (Lk 8:21). But there is only one begotten Son of the same substance and nature as the Father, God of God, Light of Light, which illumines us to wisdom (see Jn 1:9).

In God's temporal plan "our changing nature was assumed by the unchangeable Wisdom of God for our salvation and regeneration" through God's liberality.

So we believe the deeds done in time for our salvation. For example, the Son of God, born of the Virgin Mary through the power of the Holy Spirit, his death, resurrection and future coming as judge.

The Father is not at the same time the Son or vice versa (9). It is like the root and trunk of a tree—different, but one wood. So the Father and the Son are not one person, but one nature. The Father begets and the Son is begotten. And while the Father is the principle of the Son, the Son is the Image of his Father. "Insofar as he is the Son, he receives existence from his Father."

When scripture says that the Father is greater than the Son (see Jn 14:28), some feel that this refers to the Son's human nature, while "I and the Father are one" (Jn 10:30) shows the equality of the divine nature in the two persons.

"He emptied himself" (Phil 2:6) does not mean that divine wisdom changed, "but that he chose to reveal himself to men in so lowly a manner." The Son owes his existence, equality and likeness to the Father and not vice versa.

In his sermons on the Creed,[1] Augustine notes that the only Son of God is God because "God begot what he is, although he is not the person whom he begot." If he is the true Son, he is what the Father is. "Whatever begets, begets according to its kind." However, God does not beget like humans. Rather immortal begets immortal. We believe in the Father and the Son, both almighty with one will and one nature. Father and Son are inseparably one God when omnipotent begets omnipotent. On the other hand, a human son is begotten less than his father, gradually growing into equality with him. But the divine Son is begotten the perfect image of his Father, omnipotent and true.

Whatever the Father does, the Son does (see Jn 5:19). And the Son does everything the Father wills him to do. Since the Father begot his true Son, Father and Son are one God.

The only Son of God is born humbly of the Virgin Mary and the Holy Spirit. To heal the proud, God stooped down to give us his hand. "Let us take his hand and let us rise up again." But, although the Son is born in time, he is not begotten in time. How can he be begotten, since he has no beginning? The Father and Son are coeternal with no created analogy to help us out. While the Father is the fire, his Son is the brilliance of the flames, both coeval. So the Father and Son are coeval without beginning, coeternal. However, we are begotten in time and grow into perfection.

The Son of God is begotten perfect without time, coeternal with his Father, preceding all things. And he was born of the Virgin Mary at the time which he decided. Although we do not will the moment of our birth and death, this

---

1. To catechumens on the imparting of the Creed (Traditio Symboli), 2.

is not so with the Son of God, who as man hid his divine nature. "God the assumer and man the assumed, one Christ, both divine and human." Christ teaches us how to suffer by his crucifixion and he gives us hope through his resurrection. "Strive in the contest and you will be crowned." Christ ascended into heaven where he sits at the right hand of his Father and he will come to judge the living and the dead. Christ is the head of the Church, which is his body.

Son of his Father

The Word of God became man for our salvation in order that the human Christ Jesus might mediate between God and humanity. Some misinterpret scripture in thinking that the Father is greater than the Son. However, it really refers to Christ as man and not to his substance, which is coeternal with his Father (*The Trinity* 1, 7).[1]

The Son seems to be less than himself when he empties himself in order to become a servant. However, he did not lose his form of God and his equality with the Father. Thus in the form of God the Son is equal to his Father. But in the form of a slave, the man Jesus Christ is the mediator between God and humanity. In the form of God, he is greater than himself, while in the form of a slave he is less than himself. So scripture can say both that the Son is equal to the Father and also is less than the Father. The first refers to the form of God, while the second indicates his human nature.

In the form of God, he is the word through whom all things were made, but in the form of a slave, he was made of a woman under the law to redeem those under the law. "In the form of God he made man; in the form of a slave, he was made man."

Because the form of God took on the form of a slave, he is both divine and human. God takes and man is taken. However, one nature is not changed into the other. "The divinity is not changed into the creature so that it ceases to be the divinity, nor is the creature changed into the divinity so that it ceases to be a creature." The habit of Christ taken from man would not later be changed into the Godhead. So the human nature of Christ is not changed into the divine nature.

All things are subject to the Son (see 1 Cor 15:27-28; Phil 3:20-21), since the operations of the Father and the Son are inseparable. Though Christ delivers his kingdom to the Father, he does not at the same time deprive himself of it. "He is not excluding himself, because he, together with the Father, is one God." The man, Christ Jesus, the mediator between God and

---

1. Quotes in this section are from *The Trinity* (F).

humanity, reigns now among the just and will one day bring them to the face to face vision when he delivers his kingdom to his Father (see 1 Cor 13:12). All things are given to Christ by his Father. No one knows the Son, except the Father, and no one knows the Father but the Son and to whom the Son reveals him (see Mt 11:27), when he drives out all sovereignty, authority and power.

While Christ is in his secret place (see Sg 1:10), our life is hidden with Christ in God. And when Christ appears, we will be with him in glory (see Col 3:3-4).

> Jesus Christ says "I came from the Father" (Jn 16:25-28), meaning: I have not appeared in that form in which I am equal to the Father, but in another form, that is, as one less than him on account of the creature that I have assumed. (1, 7)

The Son came into the world in the form of a slave, and when he leaves the world, he takes away the form we are used to seeing. Then he goes to his Father to whom he delivers his faithful kingdom. Insofar as Christ is less than the Father, he prays; and insofar as he is equal to the Father, he listens.

When each person of the Trinity is mentioned, it is presumed that the others are also present. For example, when the Father loves us, the Son and Holy Spirit also love us.

The Son is less than his Father because he is a slave and he is less than himself because he is emptied. According to the form of God, the Son and Father are one, but according to the form of a slave, the Son is sorrowful to death. While according to the form of God, the Son is true God, according to the form of a slave, he is obedient to the cross (1, 11).

Everything the Father has, the Son has (see Jn 16:15) (1, 12). In the form of a slave, his doctrine comes from him who sent him (see Jn 7:16). When Paul said that he only knew Christ crucified (see 1 Cor 2:2), "he was speaking to those who were unable to grasp the more sublime teachings about the divinity of Christ."

In the form of God, the Son made heaven and earth, whereas in the form of a slave, he is the bridegroom. Moreover, while in the form of God he is the firstborn of all creatures, in the form of a slave he is the head of his body, the Church.

Father and Son prepare the way for us because they are one (see Mt 20:23). "He and the Father together were preparing the seats of glory for those whom they willed."

The Word of the Father is the same as the Son's. "If he speaks the Word of the Father, he speaks himself, because he himself is the Word of the Father." "That which he is, is at the same time that which he has" (Jn 5:26). The Word of God is the Son of God and the Son of God is true God and eternal life.

"I will not judge, rather the Word of the Father will judge." This means,

"I will not judge by my power as man because I am the Son of Man, but I will judge by the power of God, because I am the Son of God." "My teaching is not my own." That is, "It is mine according to the form of God, but not according to the form of a slave." "It is not my own, but his who sent me" (Jn 7:16). The doctrine of the Father is the Word of the Father, who is his only Son. "Believe in God and believe in me" (Jn 14:1), because Christ and the Father are one God.

The Son of Man in the form of a slave is also the Son of God in the form of God. He is both the crucified slave and the Lord of Glory. "For such was the assumption that made God man and man God." God was crucified "not through the power of the divinity, but through the weakness of the flesh" (2 Cor 13:4). Christ judges both as the Son of God and as the Son of Man (see Mt 25:31-32).

We will enjoy the beatific vision when the Son delivers his kingdom to his Father. And we will see the Son, too, "when the whole of creation together with that form in which the Son of God has been made the Son of Man, has been made the subject of God." For the Son also is subject to him that God may be all in all.

God exalted his Son, giving him the highest name. This refers to the Son of Man, according to whom the Son of God was raised from the dead. Because he was humbled by the cross, God exalted him. So that all will worship and confess "that the Lord Jesus Christ is in the glory of God the Father" (Phil 2:6-11).

The Son does not judge alone. Because the Father begot the Son equal to himself, the Father also judges. However, he is unseen since the Son of God appears as the Son of Man. Moreover, those who believe that Christ is the Son of God will see him also in his divinity.

In the form of a slave the Son is less than the Father and the Holy Spirit and less than himself (2, 1). And though the Son is equal to his Father, he is also from his Father, God of God, Light of Light. We speak of the Son as God of God, but we call the Father God only and not of God. For the Son has another of whom he is Son, but the Father does not have a Son of whom he is, rather he has one to whom he is Father.

"The life of the Son, as that of the Father, is unchangeable," for the operations of Father and Son are inseparable. The Son's power to work is given to him by the Father. "The Son sees the Father in this sense that he is Son precisely because he sees him." To be born of the Father is nothing else than to see him. Moreover, to see the Father working is "to work together with him." The Son can do nothing of himself because he is not from himself.

What the Son sees the Father doing, the Son also does because the Son is of the Father (see Jn 5:19). "The work of the Father and the Son is inseparable and equal, but it is from the Father to the Son. Accordingly the Son cannot do anything of himself except what he sees the Father doing." Moreover, the

"Son is not less than the Father, but he is of the Father," stressing not his inequality but rather his eternal birth from the Father. "My teaching is not my own, but his who sent me" (Jn 7:16). This can be taken two ways. First, insofar as the Son took on the form of a slave, or, secondly, in his form of God in which he is equal to the Father, but also from the Father. In either sense the Son is teaching of the Father.

When we say that the Father has given life to the Son, we mean "begot the Son, who is life." When he gave his teaching to the Son, "he begot the Son, who is teaching." And when Christ says, "My teaching is not my own, but his who sent me," he means "I am not from myself, but from him who sent me" (2, 2).

All the prophecies of the one to come are fulfilled in Jesus Christ for our salvation (4, 7). For we had fallen away form God by sin, pride and covetousness. We would come to the sinless one who died and rose for us, and hope for our own resurrection, cleansed and renewed by faith. "We are reconciled to God by our mediator so that we can adhere in the One, enjoy the One, and remain one."

> The Son of God, himself the Word of God, and himself also the mediator between God and men, the Son of Man, equal to the Father by the unity of the Godhead and our companion by the assumption of our human nature, interceded with the Father for us insofar as he was man (see 1 Tim 2:5; Rom 8:34). (4, 8)

Moreover, the Son did not keep a secret his oneness with the Father, for he said "that all may be one as we are one" (Jn 17:20-21). And Christ is also one with his Church, his mystical body. As his Godhead is consubstantial with the Father, so his disciples should be one with him, "purified through the mediator that they may be one in him."

The Father and the Son are one, not only in the equality of substance, but also in will. So Christ's disciples may also be one, "between whom and God the Son is the mediator." And they should not only be one because they possess the same nature, but also because they are of the same society of love, the Church. The Son is the mediator through whom we are reconciled to the Father (see Jn 17:23).

Our mediator, Christ, was not punished by a forced death for his sins (4, 13). Rather he died innocent and willingly. "He has been commingled into unity with the flesh by the Word of God." And he has the power to lay down his life and take it up again (see Jn 10:18).

However, the deceiver falsely portrays himself as the mediator to life. But he, "who is the true mediator of life and is alive in the spirit," was raised up from death, driving the mediator of death away from the hearts of the believers. Christ also conquered the devil's temptations so that "he might be our mediator not only by his help, but also by his example."

Although the devil was able to slay the Lord's body outwardly, his inward power over us was put to death, because our many sin chains were broken by the sinless death of the one. He willingly stripped himself and by his resurrection he protected, justified and glorified us. "The Son of God deigned to become our friend in the fellowship of death." However, the enemy imagined himself superior because he could not die and because the Lord yielded to him in his sufferings. The innocent one was put to death by the sinful one. So he might overcome and take captive the captivity of our sins, redeeming and justifying us.

Eternal life is to know the one true God and Jesus Christ whom he has sent (see 1 Jn 7:3). "Truth itself is coeternal with the Father, so he came that he might become the Son of Man," take hold of our faith and lead us to truth. "He assumed our mortality so as not to lose his own eternity." For as eternity is to that which has a beginning, so truth is related to faith. And through our faith the Lord leads us to eternal life.

What does it mean for the Son of God to be sent (4, 9)? Things brought forth from eternity are referred back to eternity. For unless inspired by great witnesses, the little ones would not believe that he "who was sent as a little one to little ones, would be great enough to make them great." Heaven and earth were made by the Son of God, and signs and wonders as well.

God sent his Son in the fullness of time, made of a woman under the law (see 1 Gal 4:4). "He is less insofar as he was made, and he was made insofar as he was sent." But since all was made through him, he is equal to him who sent him.

Christ said, "He who sees me sees the Father." Christ was both seen and not seen. "He was seen as the one who had been made and sent. He was not seen as the one through whom all things were made." Though he was accepted in the flesh through faith, the Word reserved that the mind, cleansed by faith, might contemplate him in eternity.

Even if the Father sends the Son, this does not prevent us from believing that "the Son is equal, consubstantial and coeternal with the Father, and yet that the Son has been sent by the Father"—not as though one is greater and the other less. Father and Son, Begetter and Begotten, Sender and Sent. The Son is from the Father and not vice versa.

The Son is sent that the Word might be made flesh and so fulfill the prophecies. The Word was sent in order to become man, but was not sent as one unequal to the Father, even though from the Father.

The Word of the Father is his Son, but also his Wisdom and a pure emanation of the glory of God. "That which emanates and that from which it emanated are one and the same substance," light from eternal light. Brightness is coeternal with the light, and though it issues from the light, it is not greater or less.

"The Word of God is sent by him of whom it is the Word," and sent by him of whom it was born. The Son was sent because the Word was made flesh to be apprehended in time by men and women. What is born of the eternal one is eternal, but what is sent in time is apprehended by each one. When the Word was sent forth in time and grasped by each mind, he could not be seen by bodily senses. Begetter and Begotten are one; Sender and Sent are one; Father and Son are one; and Father, Son and Holy Spirit are one, since the Spirit is the Spirit of the Father and the Son. Unity is the theme of John's gospel. Father, Son and the Christians are one (see Jn 6:3). Father and Son are one God, wise and great. The Father is not better than his Son in greatness, eternity or wisdom, since the Son is equal to his Father in everything that is predicated of the substance of God.

Immense Creator in a Tiny Baby[1]

Augustine's friend Volusion asks how the founder of the universe can be hidden in the body of a tiny baby? And how could he rule the world from such a site? Moreover, did he give any indication of his majesty? Augustine responds that God did not transfer the ruling of the universe to a tiny baby. God is a spiritual presence, not a material one. So he is everywhere without being confined. We think it is impossible that the Word of God who made all became man without destroying his immortality, eternity or providence or without leaving his Father.

The Word of God "remains as he is, and he is everywhere totally present." He comes in revelation and goes away hidden. So a light is present to the sighted, while it is absent to the blind. The Word of God is present everywhere like the word of man which is heard entirely by each one who listens.

There should be no fear that the immense God cannot fit into a small infant. For his greatness is in power, not in mass. Thus he gives more brains to an ant than to an ass. Moreover, from a small part of our brain our entire body is governed. "He who is not small in small things produces great things from the least."

So the greatness of God's power felt no narrowness in the womb of the virgin by an intrinsic birth, taking on a human soul and body. "And it chose to better humankind without suffering any diminution itself, deigning to take the name of humanity from man, while granting him a share in the divinity."

The Son took on human nature with all its needs and feelings. What if Christ had suddenly appeared full grown without any infancy or youth, without sleeping or eating? Would he be a real man? But he came as a mediator between God and humanity, two natures in one person, raising the common to the heights, while bringing the uncommon to the common.

---

1. Quotes from Letter 137 to Volusian, a Christian judge (412).

He who does not need seeds to make seeds, does not need seeds to make a human body. "What began outside of time, took growth in the course of time." In the beginning the Word who made time chose time to become flesh, drawing humanity near to God.

As soul and body make up one person, so God and man are one person in Christ, by taking on the soul and body of man. It is easier for two incorporeal things to mix than one corporeal and one incorporeal.

The Word of God and the Son of God are coeternal with the Father, sharing the same power and wisdom of God. From the highest end of rational creation to the lowest end of material creation, everywhere present, but here in a mode more present. "This Word took on human nature and thereby became one Jesus Christ, the mediator between God and humanity," immortal in his divinity where he is equal to the Father and mortal according to his human nature.

Christ is a master and helper toward salvation, confirming the prophets, philosophers and others. By his incarnation he told them he was not far off, yet "so close to their affectionate desire that he became man and to be united to him." Though the whole man was joined to him, God was not changed. He is our help in overcoming lust and the remains of our sins.

Miracles are really small things for God to do, since the prophets did them. However, the prophets foretold the coming of Christ, who not only did all the things which he had done before through human beings, but also was born of a virgin, died, rose and ascended into heaven.

Why did not Christ create a new world as proof of his divinity? Actually his virgin birth, death, resurrection and ascension are mightier wonders than the creation of the world.

Christ, Founder of the City of God

In his *The City of God* (9, 15)[1] Augustine notes that miserable men and women need a mediator who is both human and divine, "in order that by the intervention of his blessed mortality, human beings could be led from their mortal misery to blessed immortality." "Because he is incarnate not by a diminution of his death, but rather by assuming frail flesh, which he raised from the dead."

What is his mediation? That human beings "should not remain forever subject to the death of the flesh." So our mediator must have a passing mortality and an enduring beatitude, conformed temporarily to mortals, but transported from death to life.

The devil is an immoral and mean mediator, luring us from the true savior,

1. Quotes in this section are from *The City of God* (413-27) (F).

the uncreated Lord. The Word of God is our mediator because he is human, and as man he shows us the way to the supreme good so we can share in his divinity.

Christ is the firm foundation of the Christian Catholic (21, 26). A good basement determines the sound construction of a building. The person "who has Christ for his or her foundation is the one whose heart possesses Christ," so that nothing is preferred to Christ.

Christ is not the founder of the city of God in the same sense that Romulus built Rome (22, 6). "For this city does not believe Christ to be God because it was founded by him, but, on the contrary, the city came to be founded because people believed he was God."

Rome worshipped its founder in a temple, while "this 'Jerusalem' offered its faith in Christ, its founder, as God in the hope that on this foundation the city might be built and consecrated." Rome believed that Romulus was a God because they loved him. However, "Jerusalem loved its founder because it believed that he was God." "Our true faith led to a love of a truly divine founder."

Prophets and miracles prove that Christ is God, not so in the case of Romulus. Moreover, the Christian martyrs also testify that Christ is God.

Enchiridion: Son of God, Son of Man[1]

The Word of God was made flesh so that we might believe in the only Son of God, the Father almighty, born of the Holy Spirit and the Virgin Mary. But the divinity is not changed into flesh (10).

Christ Jesus, the Son of God, is both God and man, God before all ages and man in our age. "God because he is the Word of God; man because in the unity of his person there was joined to the Word a body and rational soul." In God, the Son and Father are one, but in his manhood, the Son is less than his Father (2, 21). The Son of God became the Son of Man, two natures, but one Christ.

The Son of God emptied himself, taking on the form of a servant, without at the same time diminishing his Godhead. "He became less and remained equal, being both in one." As the Word of God he is equal to the Father, but as human he is less. However, he is one person who is both the Son of God and the Son of Man. God without a beginning, man with a beginning are one Lord Jesus Christ.

"What had the human nature in the man Christ deserved that it should be taken up into the unity of the person of the only Son of God?" Did he, as man, deserve divinity? Augustine opposes adoptionism. Rather "from the

1. Quotes in this section are from the *Enchiridion* (421-22) (F).

moment in which he began to be man, he was nothing other than the Son of God, and the only Son of God."

He was the Word of God who took on human nature and flesh, yet remained true God. Just as we join our body and soul in one person, so Christ joins the Word and man. Moreover, we are justified from our sins by the same grace which enabled Christ to be free from sin.

Augustine Preaches on the Incarnation: A Speechless Child and the Eternal Word[1]

Could God have assumed flesh without at the same time changing into flesh (S 184)? "He took upon himself what he was not, yet he remained what he was." Though he came in the form of man, he did not depart from his Father. Preserving his divine nature, he appeared to us in our human nature.

Truth Eternal was born as man. "Truth, holding the world in place, has sprung from the earth so that he might be carried in the hands of a woman." He whom heaven cannot contain was placed in a manger for us, freeing us from our sins (S 185).

The Word became flesh. However, the Word was not destroyed when it was clothed with human nature. "Rather the flesh, to avoid destruction, drew near the Word" (S 186).

"The same one who is human is God and the same one who is God is human, not by the confusion of natures, but by the unity of person." The Son of God is coeternal with the Father, but, born of a virgin, he became the Son of Man. Thus humanity is added to divinity, without making a quaternity in lieu of the Trinity.

"The Word became flesh, without the divinity being changed into something lower." The gospel says that the Word became flesh, yet the Word is God (Jn 1:14, 1). "The Son of God became the Son of Man by taking on himself a lower nature without changing his higher nature, by receiving what he was not, not by losing what he was."

No one denies that the Son of Man was born of a virgin. To be born of a virgin, the Son of God

> assumed the form of a servant and became the Son of Man, remaining what he was and taking upon himself what he was not, beginning to exist in that, as man, he was less than the Father, yet always existing insofar as he and the Father are one. (Phil 2:6-8)

Equal to the Father, he humbled himself, taking on the form of a servant. And he died on the cross under the form of the Son of Man. He was always

1. From Augustine's Christmas and Easter Sermons (F).

the Son of God, but became the Son of David. "Born of the Father without
the limits of time, he was born of a mother on this day."

Christmas signifies the work of Christ, renewing our inner soul. When
creation was at peace, the eternal Creator was created in time. The Lord who
made all things was made flesh amid all the works of his own hands. "The
manifestor of his Father and Creator of his mother, the Son of God, born of
his Father without a mother, and the Son of Man, born of a mother without
a father" (S 187).

The Word of God, existing before all time was made flesh, existing only
for an allotted time. Creator of the sun, he was created under the light of the
sun. Maker of heaven and earth, he was brought forth on earth, overshadowed
by the heavens. "Unspeakably wise, yet wisely speechless; filling the whole
world, while lying in a manger."

His greatness as God is not lessened by his insignificance, nor was his
smallness crushed by his might. Moreover, when he took on human form, he
did not stop his divine actions. So the Son of God was not changed into the
Son of Man, but the divine nature was perfectly preserved when he took on
human nature. Remaining the Son of God, he became the Son of Man.

Our own word comes out in our speech, yet it is not changed into speech.
Though our voice comes out in our spoken language, our inner word and
thought remain the same. However, our word and thought are ephemeral,
while the Word of God is eternal.

The Word did not give up his eternity by becoming flesh. Rather he gave
immortality to flesh. Moreover, he did not cling to his divinity so as not to
empty himself in order to take on the form of a servant.

While our body and soul make for us one human nature, for him they make
only his visible nature, for if he had not a body and soul he would still be
God. "Remaining God, he became human," what he was not before. So he
has two natures. "The Father is greater than I," signifies his human nature,
while "I and the Father are one," refers to his divine nature. "Hiding what he
was, he showed forth only what he had become." Remaining God, he became
man so that the Son of Man can rightly be called Emmanuel (God with us).

Greater than Mary, he is born of Mary. Son of David, he is Lord of David.
Seed of Abraham, he is exalted before Abraham. Fashioner of the earth, he
was fashioned on earth. Creator of heaven, he was created as man under the
light of heaven.

We do not form our words in the same way that the Father begot the Word.
"For God begot God, but the Begetter and the Begotten are one and the same
God." God, who made the world which passes, remains God. "He by whom
all things were made was made by no one."

Human pride and disobedience in the garden of Eden were replaced by
divine humility and obedience. In obedience he became mortal so that we
can live.

"He created all things, yet he (as man) was created among all things. He made the day and he came into the day. He is the Lord Christ, existing without a beginning eternally with his Father, yet he has a birthday" (S 189). Without the human generation of the Word, we would not have divine regeneration. "He was born so that we might be born again." While Mary carried him in her womb, we cherish him in our hearts. Christ has a twofold generation: eternally born of the Father without a mother; but born in time of a mother without a father. He who fills the world found no room at the inn. "Placed in a manger, he became our food." His birthday was chosen on the solstice when the light conquers the darkness. For then Christ the light overcomes the shadows of sin (S 190).

The infant Jesus "is both a speechless child and he is the Word." The divine shepherd appeared to the Bethlehem shepherds. His human weakness was from his mother, while his divine majesty was from his Father. Living a brief span of days on earth, he is the Eternal Day, born of the Eternal Day, God of God, Light of Light.

From the everlasting day of eternity to the day of man. "There God is with God, here he is God and man. There he is the Light of Light, here the Light which enlightens every man" (S 191). There he sits at the right hand of the Father, here he lies in a manger. There feeding the angels, while here he is a hungry child. There doing good, here suffering evil. There never dying, here rising from the dead to give eternal life.

"God became man so that man might become God," taking on the form of a servant that we might turn to God. The Founder of heaven came to earth so that we might rise from earth to heaven. "In the bosom of his Father he existed before all the cycles of ages; born of an earthly mother, he entered upon the course of years on this day."

Man's Maker became man to be nourished at Mary's breasts. The Divine Bread would be hungry and the Divine Fountain thirst. The Way would take an earthly journey. Truth would be accused of falsehood. The Judge of the living and the dead would be judged. Justice would be treated unjustly. Courage would suffer weakness, Security wounded, while Life dies.

The Son of God before the ages became the Son of Man in recent years to become an innocent sufferer.

Christ died for us. The Just One for sinners; Master for slaves; Free One for captives, Physician for the sick; Happy for the depressed; Rich for the needy; Seeker for the lost; Redeemer for the sold; Shepherd for sheep, Creator for creatures (S 220).

Preserving what he had, he gave up what he became. Hiding as God, he appeared as man. Giving life by his power, yet dying in infirmity. "Unchangeable in divinity, yet susceptible to pain in the flesh" (Rom 4:25).

Christ, our Passover offering, is sacrificed only once, though we celebrate it yearly. The Lord Jesus Christ made one day sad by his death and another glorious by his resurrection (S 221). Our Passover is not observed by killing a sheep, but by the sacrifice of the Shepherd, Christ. And it is fitting that he rose at night because he came to illuminate our darkness.

What was Christ before he became man? Before Abraham, I am (see Jn 8:57, 58). The Word was God (see Jn 1:1). Through him heaven and earth were made. But the Word was not made. While our words created by our thought and voice soon fade, the divine Word is eternal (S 225).

How is the Word of God, the Creator of all, in Mary's womb? Did he leave heaven? "In order that man might eat the bread of angels, the Lord of angels became man." However, God's Word did not leave heaven. "That womb received what the world could not contain," but he was not made smaller. "Just as my word assumes sound, through which it is heard, so the Word assumed flesh in order to be seen."

Augustine is just an ordinary human being, trying to speak about the great God, who is such that we cannot describe him. Yet we ought not to be silent. So Augustine feeds crumbs from the Lord's table to his flock, whom Christ has regenerated and filled with the Holy Spirit.

The resurrection of our Lord, Jesus Christ, is a new life for those who believe in him, and the sacrament of his death and resurrection. Life came from death. For the Fountain of Life, from which we drink, freely drank the chalice of suffering (S 231).

Sin is the father of death, which is the penalty of sin. Though innocent, our Lord Jesus Christ came to die. "By sharing with us the penalty without the sin, he canceled both the penalty and the sin." While on the cross he showed the destruction of our old man; but "he rose again so that he might point out the newness of our life." When he rose on the eighth day, he renewed us also. So in our baptism we rise again with Christ. If the Christian "used to live badly and is not now doing so, he has died. And if he is now living well, he has risen again."

Christ came to share our misery. Scourged and nailed to a cross, he rose on the third day. And when his work was finished, the Lord raised him up to his right hand.

He promised his life for us, inviting us to share his life that never dies, the abode of angels, friendship of the Trinity and the eternal banquet. To me and my life his death is a pledge of his gift of life. But we have to die with Christ in order to live with him. We must come to Christ and live with him who died for us.

Our faith is based on the resurrection of Christ (S 233). While others believe in his passion, "Christians alone believe in his resurrection." Though the passion of Christ shares the sorrows of our life, his resurrection shows the joys of the future life. Christ, the Fountain of Life, came and died for us and his salvation does not pass away.

Jesus Christ called himself the Son of Man to remind us of Adam who was not the Son of man. While man brought death, the Son of Man gives us life. Man sins, but the Son of Man remits sin. Man is in slavery, but the Son of Man frees him. Man is condemned, but the Son of Man acquits.

Our salvation is not found here. "This salvation came hither and here found our death." The Son of God came as a merchant, bringing a great gift, but only finding birth and death. "He came from heaven, from his Father, yet he was born a mortal," born of Mary through the Holy Spirit in the likeness of our sinful flesh (Rom 8:3).

He came as a savior, conquering death by his cross, taking death upon himself and defeating it. Moreover, what has taken place in the head, will also happen for his members.

By his death Christ brings us into being, so by his resurrection we grow into maturity (S 236). Our life is foreshadowed by his death. Buried with Christ in our baptism, we walk with him in a new life (see Lk 24:17-28). The innocent death of Christ frees us from our sins. Then we can be justified by his resurrection. However, even some of his disciples doubted his rising.

At Emmaus Jesus entered the home of his disciples and was recognized in the breaking of the bread. So we should receive our fellow Christians as Christ. For he "is in need in his followers." "He who is needy in his followers draws all the needy to himself," toward their final glory (Lk 24:37-39) (S 237).

Some say that the divine Christ is spirit and not flesh, since the spirit is superior to the flesh. But Augustine replies that Christ is both spirit and flesh, God and man, body and soul.

For our sake he poured out his blood, "enduring what he had not merited." Thus the Word of God made human redeemed us.

What is this Word of God? It cannot be uttered by the word of man. He fills the world and the virgin's womb. However, he is not spread out physically over the world or confined to the womb. "He who created the whole man and redeemed the whole man, assumed the whole man and thus freed the whole man."

Be avaricious for Christ. For the Father says, "I made my rich Son poor for your sake." He who made gold, silver and gems became poor for us (S 239).

The Lord Christ, the Wisdom of God, has come to be mediator between the just God and unjust man, "possessing his humanity from below and his justice from above." And so he is placed midway. If he were completely divine, he would not belong here. And, on the other hand, if he were completely human, he would stay here. If we believe in our mediator and are faithful to him, we will join him in heaven (S 240).

In this chapter we have seen some of Augustine's teachings on the Son of God made human, true God and true man, who, taking on our sinful flesh, died an innocent death for our redemption. The immense God chose to enter the world through the humble womb of his virgin mother. In the following chapter we will see more of Augustine's mariology. For Mary is both mother of Christ and also mother of his Church.

III.

HE WAS MADE MAN IN THE MOTHER
WHOM HE HIMSELF HAD MADE

(Sermon 191)

Virgin Mother of God

It seems that Mary was honored as the virgin mother of Christ from earliest times. For example, Ignatius of Antioch (see Eph 19:1). Also many saw Mary as the second Eve, whose life-giving obedience overcomes her predecessor's deadly disobedience.[1] Mary also is called Jesse's rod.[2]

Origen and the Alexandrians named Mary the mother of God long before she was declared so by the Council of Ephesus (431). And Tertullian notes[3] that the Word of God took on his stainless flesh from the pure virgin, the new Eve. Moreover, he contradicts the Gnostics who teach that Mary is just a channel of the incarnation of God's Son who is conceived of a virgin and born of a mother. So Jesus' "brothers" are the younger children of Mary (chapter 7).

Alexander of Alexandria, writing against the Arians, calls Mary, Theotokos, or God-bearing. She is Theotokos because Christ's divine and human natures make one person, whose mother is Mary. Furthermore, she is a perpetual virgin, so that Christ is her only child.[4]

Theophilus of Alexandria writes that Mary is Theotokos, redemptrix and advocate, interceding for us in heaven. Mary is our ambassadress who places our petitions before her Son. She is virgin mother, queen, mother of God, Theotokos.[5] So Mary is honored especially in Egypt as God's mother. She who brought her Son to Egypt to escape Herod, is adopted by the Copts as their queen and mother.

Cyril of Jerusalem also says that Mary is truly the mother of God and not just a channel.[6] Since there are many miraculous births recorded in the Bible

---

1. Justin, *Trypho* 94; Irenaeus, *Against the Heretics* 3, 22, 4.
2. Irenaeus, *Proof of the Apostolic Teaching* 59.
3. Tertullian, *The Flesh of Christ* 17, 18.
4. Athanasius, *Letter to Epictetus* 5; *Against the Arians* 2, 70.
5. W. H. Worrel, ed., *The Coptic Manuscripts in the Freer Collection* (New York: Macmillan, 1923), 359-79.
6. Cyril of Jerusalem, *Catechetical Lectures* 4, 9; 12, 27.

and in Greek literature, why cannot Christ be born of a virgin by the Holy Spirit? Mary is the Christian model of virginity and chastity. The Cappadocian doctors, Gregory of Nazianzen and Gregory of Nyssa also praise Mary Theotokos.[1] The latter points out that as a virgin mother gave birth to Christ, so our virgin souls can generate Christ spiritually. John Chrysostom asks how the Infinite One can enter a tiny womb? How can Mary be both a virgin and a mother? There are many unanswered questions here. But Mary is Jesus' mother because she did his Father's will. John Chrysostom does not use Theotokos like the Alexandrians or Christotokos like the Antiochenes, but he staunchly defends Mary's perpetual virginity.[2] As the Church grew, she saw more clearly Mary's place in redemption as the second Eve, Theotokos and coredemptrix.

Ambrose and Jerome

Ambrose, bishop of Milan, studied the mariology of the Greek Fathers. He had his hands full fighting off the Arian Goths who denied the total divinity of Christ. He also tried to discourage his flock from worshipping the popular Roman goddess, Kybele or Magna Mater (the Greek earth queen, daughter of Gaea).

Ambrose's mariology is closely tied to his christology. Christ is both true God and true man. While his eternal generation is from his Father, his human birth is from his virgin mother. Using Old Testament metaphors (On the Holy Spirit 2, 5), he calls the family of Jews Jesse's root, while Mary is Jesse's rod and Jesus is the flower. Though the Son of God received his human flesh from the Virgin Mary, "Mary was the temple of God, not the god of the temple. Thus he alone is to be adored who was operating in the temple."

Ambrose stresses the union of the divine and human in the incarnation. "The same is of the Father in the one way and from the virgin in the other." Many things are in Christ according to nature and many things are beyond nature. According to the body he was in the womb, born, nursed in the crib, etc.

> But beyond this condition, the virgin conceived; the virgin bore him, that you might believe that it was God who renewed nature, and it was man who was born of man according to nature.[3]

Though the cause of Christ's generation is different from ours, "nevertheless, the flesh of Christ is of one nature with all" (chapter 9).

Christ's birth did not change Mary's nature, but rather established a new

1. Gregory of Nazianzen, L 101; Gregory of Nyssa, *On Virginity.*
2. John Chrysostom, *Homilies on Matthew* 4, 6; 12, 46-49.
3. Ambrose, The Sacrament of the Incarnation of the Lord, chap. 5 (F).

method of generation. "She contributed her own from her womb in an unusual manner, but in a usual function." So Mary's and Jesus' nature is the same according to the flesh and not unlike that of his human brothers and sisters (see Hb 2:17).

Though the Greeks called Mary Theotokos from the time of Origen, Ambrose rarely used the title Dei Genetrix to save confusion with Kybele, the famous Magna Mater of Roman religion. However, he has no doubts that Mary is the mother of God, our salvation and our life.

Ambrose also says that Mary is a type of the Church, a betrothed, spotless virgin (*On Luke* 2, 7). In the womb of the Church we are conceived by the Holy Spirit as Christ was conceived in the womb of Mary.

Hilda Graef comments,[1] "Everything enacted in the Church was first enacted in Mary." "Mary is inseparable from the Church, and the Church from Mary, for in her womb the mystical body of Christ was formed with his physical body." "Mary is the mother of all Christians, as the Church is our mother. Both, mystically speaking, are one." Mary is the Church in germ. For when she conceived Christ, she conceived all who were to be his own.

For Ambrose, Mary is the perfect woman, mother of God, model of virgins, prefigured in the Old Testament as a pure cloud, light, Jesse's rod, etc.[2] Some call Ambrose the father of Western mariology.

Mary's perfection is a prerequisite for her divine motherhood. And since she carried the whole mystical body of Christ in her womb, she is inseparable from his Church.

Jerome (342-420), foremost scripture scholar of his time, links his mariology with his scriptural exegesis and his doctrine of the primacy of virginity, of which Mary's perpetual purity is the paradigm.

Jerome had little patience with the apocryphal stories about Mary and the holy family, for example, the Protoevangelium of James. So he did not accept the tale of Joseph as an old widower with children. Rather he is a young strong protector and guardian of Mary, while the brothers of the Lord are cousins or nephews.

Jerome believes that Mary was a virgin before and after the birth of Jesus, who passed through closed doors as he did after his resurrection from the dead. Jerome's exegesis and especially his use of Old Testament figures stimulated Ambrose's study of Mary.

Augustine: Mary, Virgin and Mother

Like his Roman predecessors, Augustine avoids the term Dei Genetrix

---

1. H. Graef, *Mary, A History of Doctrine and Devotion*, vol. 1 (New York: Sheed and Ward, 1963), 85-86.
2. H. Graef, *Mary*, 88.

because of the pagan devotion to the Magna Mater. Augustine's mariology was influenced by both Ambrose and Jerome.

In 393 Augustine preached to the African bishops on the place of Mary in God's plan, whereby his Son became man through the Holy Spirit and the virgin mother.

He took upon himself a complete human nature within the virgin's womb, dwelling within his mother's inviolate body and leaving it inviolate at his departure. (*On Faith and Creed,* chap. 4)

In the incarnation of his Son, God ennobled both sexes, by possessing a male nature and being born of a woman.

Christ seems to spurn his mother at the wedding feast at Cana (see Jn 2:4). As God he had no mother, for his hour had not yet come. But as man hanging on the cross, he acknowledged his earthly mother, commending her to the care of his apostle John (see Jn 19:26-27).

And how about the occasion when Jesus did not want to be bothered by his mother and brothers (see Mt 12:48)? He seems to be teaching the priority of the apostolate over relationships.

There is no danger of Christ's divinity being contaminated in the human body of Mary, when the spiritual Word of God took on a human body and soul. "Through the medium of the majesty of the Word he takes up a more hidden abode, removed from the frailty of a human body."

Augustine further explains Mary's position in the incarnation to his catechumens, noting the humility of the Son of God, born of a virgin mother and the Holy Spirit, in order to lift up men and women (*Expositions to Catechumens,* chap. 3).

Christ's nativity is both lowly and lofty, lowly as a man born of a woman, but lofty "because he was born of a virgin. A virgin conceived, a virgin brought forth, and after bringing forth, remained a virgin."

In his *Christian Combat* (chap. 22) he says that it is fitting that the Savior of men and women came as a man born of a woman. Moreover, it is not difficult for God who created the whole world out of nothing to make a dove for the Holy Spirit and to form a human body in Mary's womb without the aid of a human father.

Mary is the model of virginity (*On Virginity,* 22). "Christ, the Son of a virgin and the spouse of virgins, born bodily from a virginal womb, can by a virginal espousal help us spiritually." Since the whole Church is the virgin spouse of Christ (see 2 Cor 11:2), virgins should be honored in the Church, that virginity "which the whole Church, imitating the mother of her Spouse and Lord, preserves in the faith." Like Mary, the Church is both mother and virgin.

Mary bore the head of the body in the flesh; the Church bears the members of that head in the spirit. In neither does virginity impede fecundity; and in neither does fecundity destroy virginity.

When Jesus' relatives wanted to see him at Capernaum, he said his true mother and brothers are those who do the will of his Father. "Thus Mary was more blessed in accepting the faith of Christ than in conceiving the flesh of Christ" (chapter 3). Moreover, when people praised his mother's womb and breasts, Jesus replied, "Rather blessed are they who hear the word of God and keep it" (Lk 11:27-28). "Even her maternal relationship would have done Mary no good unless she had borne Christ more happily in her heart than in her flesh."

Mary's virginity is more beautiful and pleasing because Christ "in his conception did not himself take away that which he was preserving from violation by man." Before his conception Jesus chose a consecrated virgin (chapter 4). When Mary replied to the angel "I know not man," she spoke of her vow of virginity. However, according to Jewish custom she was espoused to Joseph.

As a model of virginity, Mary consecrated her body to God, "while she was still ignorant of what she would conceive, by her own free choice and not by compulsion." "Even in that woman in whom he took upon himself the nature of a slave, he desired virginity to be free."

Vowed virgins should not be anxious because they cannot have children. "For virginity could appropriately bear him alone who in his birth could not have an equal" (chapter 5). The Christ Child born of the Virgin Mary, is the glory of all vowed virgins. "They, together with Mary, are the mothers of Christ, if they do the will of the Father." Mary is preeminently and happily the mother of Christ, because she does perfectly the will of the Father (see Mt 12:50).

Holy men and women Christians are the brothers and sisters of Christ, coheirs of heaven and the Church is their mother, bringing forth the faithful through the grace of God. A holy soul can be a mother of Christ. Thus Mary, obedient to the Father, "is merely the mother of Christ in the body, but both sister and mother in the spirit."

Mary is mother of us, who are Christ's members. "Because she has cooperated by her charity that the faithful, who are members of that head, might be born in the Church. Indeed, she is the mother of the head himself in the body." The head should be born of a virgin according to the flesh to show that "his members would be born according to the spirit, of a virgin, the Church."

Mary alone is mother and virgin both in spirit and in body, both mother of Christ and virgin of Christ. So the Church in her saints is "wholly the mother of Christ, wholly the virgin of Christ in spirit." In the body of the Church some are virgins of Christ, while others are mothers, but not mothers of Christ.

However, both holy virgins and mothers "are spiritually mothers of Christ because they do the will of his Father." Mothers give birth to Adams and Eves who will become members of the body of Christ through baptism.

How can the immense God fit into Mary's small womb (L 137)?

That very greatness of his power, which feels no narrowness in narrow quarters, enriched the virgin's womb, not by an externally caused, but by an intrinsic childbirth.

Taking on our humanity, he gave us a share in his divinity. In his *The Trinity* (4, 5) Augustine studies the numerology of Christ's gestation in Mary's womb. Christ often spoke of his body as a temple, which he would raise up again three days after it was destroyed. Though it took 46 years to build the Jerusalem temple, Christ's body was formed in 46 times 6 or 276 days in Mary's womb. He was conceived on March 25, the same day he died, and he was born on December 25. Moreover, the womb of the virgin where no mortal person was begotten corresponds to the new tomb in which Christ was buried.

God chose to assume human nature in order to conquer the enemy of the human race, "to take it from a virgin, whose conception, the spirit, not the flesh, the faith, not the passion, preceded" (Lk 1:26-28) (13, 18). "The holy virginity was fecundated by believing, not by lying together." Christ, the sinless man, was conceived and born to save us from our sins.

Jesus came to the Cana wedding as a bridegroom (*On John* 8, 4). The womb of Mary in which he became the head of the Church was his bridal chamber, from which he came forth in joy.

At Cana Mary asked a miracle of her Son. "But he, about to perform divine works, so far did not recognize a human womb."

That in me which works a miracle was not born of you. For you gave not birth to my divine nature. But because my weakness was born of you, I will recognize you at the time when that same weakness shall hang upon the cross. (9)

Christ had always known his mother in predestination. "Even before he was born of her; even before, as God, he created her, and as man he was to be created, he knew her as his mother."

But in a certain hour of divine mystery he does not acknowledge her and in the future hour of mystery on the cross he will recognize her, "when that to which she gave birth was dying." "That by which Mary was made did not die, but that which was made *of* Mary. Not the eternity of the divine nature, but the weakness of the flesh was dying."

"Though he was God and the Lord of heaven, he came by a mother who was a woman." He was Lord of heaven and of Mary. But he was also her son. "The same, both the Lord of Mary and the Son of Mary; Creator of Mary and created from Mary." Though he was the son of David and Mary, he is also their Lord according to his divinity. And their son according to the flesh.

Jesus' mother, brothers and disciples walk over to Capernaum (see Jn 2:12-21) (*On John* 10, 2). Who are these brothers of Jesus? They could have the same father, the same mother or the same father and mother; or they could be cousins. However, Mary did not give birth a second time. "The kinsmen of Mary, of whatever degree, are the brothers of the Lord." Thus Lot was called Abraham's brother. Moreover, an uncle or the son of a sister can be called one's brother. Augustine notes, "When you know this rule you will find that all the blood relatives of Mary are the brethren of Christ." Jesus' disciples are also called brothers as were the early Christians named brothers and sisters in the Lord.

Jesus asks: who are my mother and brothers? Those who do the will of my Father (see Mt 12:46-50). This also applies to Mary, "because she did the will of the Father. What the Lord magnified in her was that she did the will of the Father, not that flesh gave birth to flesh."

When people admired Mary's holy womb, Jesus stressed rather her obedience to the Father (Lk 11:27). "Even my mother, whom you have called happy, is happy in that she keeps the word of God," not because in her the Word of God became flesh and dwelt among us. "But because she keeps that same Word of God, by which she was made and which in her was made flesh." So we should not exult in our temporal children but rather because we are joined in spirit with God.

When Pelagius claimed that it was not uncommon for the saints to be sinless, Augustine responds that there is no question of sin in Mary alone (*Nature and Grace* 42).

> What abundance of grace for overcoming sin in every particular was conferred on her, who had the merit to conceive and bear him, who undoubtedly had no sin. (1 Jn 3:5)

Other saints, if heard now, would readily admit their faults.

Writing on faith (*Enchiridion*, chap. 10), Augustine reaffirms that we believe in the Son of God born of Mary and the Holy Spirit. He was not born of the union of man and woman, rather he was conceived by the virgin's faith. Moreover, "if her virginity were marred even in his being born, then he would not have been born of a virgin." This doctrine is taught by the Church, "which in imitation of his mother daily brings forth members of his body and remains a virgin."

Christmas Sermons

In Augustine's Christmas sermons (184-96) (F) we find the epitome of his mariology. "This day on which the virgin, true and inviolate mother, gave birth to him who became visible for our sake and by whom she herself was created" (S 186).

> "A virgin conceives, yet she remains a virgin." It was fitting for God to be born thus, when he deigned to become man. Such did he make her, who was born from her. He existed before she was created. And

because he was omnipotent, he was able to become man, while remaining what he was.

"He created his own mother when he was with the Father; and when he was born of that mother, he remained in his Father." In the incarnation human flesh was drawn to the Word and not vice versa. So Christ is man and God, body and soul, Son of God and Son of Man. In paradise eloquent man named all the creatures. Yet, "for your sake, your Creator lay speechless and did not even call his mother by her name." By his obedience, he reversed our disobedience (S 188).

We celebrate with joy the day when Mary brought forth the Savior, the day "on which the one, joined in marriage, brought forth the Creator of the union; and a virgin gave birth to the prince of virgins." Though Mary was given to a husband, she is not a mother by that husband, since she was a virgin before marriage, in marriage, when with child and while nursing her child. Christ was able to give both fertility and virginity to Mary. And "the holy Church as a virgin celebrates today the child-bearing of a virgin."

Paul betrothed the chaste virgin Church to Christ (2 Cor 11:2). "Christ, intending to establish virginity in the heart of the Church, preserved it first in the body of Mary." "The Church could not be a virgin unless she first found the Son of the virgin as a Spouse to whom she might be given."

On Christmas day the Word of God was born, clothed with the flesh of the Virgin Mary. "He was formed in her whom he himself had formed." "Though he gave her fertility, he did not mar her virginity." Mary sprang from Adam, who came from the earth. So Truth sprang from the earth (Ps 84:12) (S 189). He is the eternal Son of God, yet he has a birthday. "If the Word had not had human generation, we would not have acquired divine regeneration."

His mother carried him in her womb; let us carry him in our hearts. The virgin was heavy with the incarnate Christ; may our hearts be heavily freighted with belief in Christ. The virgin brought forth the Savior; may our souls bring forth salvation. (S 189)

Christ and Mary overcame the sin of Adam and Eve. "The nativity of the Lord encouraged both sexes to hope for salvation," because the God-Man was born of a holy virgin (S 190).

"The Church, therefore, imitating the mother of her Lord in mind, though not in body, is both mother and virgin" (S 191). Augustine asks the virgins of his Church to "rejoice now and celebrate with all solemnity the fecundity of the virgin on this day."

She in whose footsteps you are following had no human intercourse when she conceived. She remained a virgin when she brought forth her child.

Imitate her as far as you can in the preservation of your virginity.

Mary alone can be both mother and virgin through the power of the Lord. "It was fitting that the only-begotten Son of God alone should become the Son of Man in this way." "You have gained as a spouse of your heart him whom you could not bring forth as your child in the flesh." When he preserves your virginity in his loving embrace, consider how to please your spouse (see 1 Cor 32-35).

Augustine addresses the whole Church, the chaste spouse of Christ. Imitate Mary in your inner souls, for who believes, brings forth Christ. "In your souls let fertility abound and virginity be preserved."

"We marvel at the childbearing of a virgin," trying hard to explain it to non-believers (S 192). How could she conceive a child without a man and remain a virgin even in parturition? However, God's power can do whatever he wants. So he can be born in whatever way he chooses.

"He who was born as the only Son of his mother, was already the only Son of his Father. He was fashioned as man by the mother whom he himself had made." Though he existed eternally with his Father, he took on a temporal life with his mother. "Created by his mother after his mother, he was uncreated by his Father before all time. Without him, his Father never existed, and without him his mother never would have existed." Augustine calls Mary the model of virgins, while Anna is the paradigm of widows and Elizabeth of conjugal chastity.

To the virgins he advises to conceive Christ in their hearts and show him forth in good works.

> Let your heart accomplish in the law of Christ what Mary's womb wrought in the flesh of Christ. How are you not included in the childbearing of the virgin, since you are members of Christ?

While Mary gave birth to the head, the virgins bring forth his members.

The Church, like Mary, is both mother and virgin. The spouse of Christ, she procreates diverse members "of him whose body and spouse she is." She is like the virgin, because in the midst of many she is the mother of unity. Christ, the Mediator, "born of his Father, he created his mother. Formed as a man in his mother, he glorified his Father." The only Son of his Father without a mother and only Son of his mother without man's cooperation (S 195).

> He, the Son of holy Mary and the Spouse of the holy Church, has made the Church like his mother, since he made it a mother for us and kept it a virgin for himself.

"The Church, then, like Mary, has inviolate integrity and incorrupt fecundity." What Mary merited physically, the Church guards spiritually. While Mary brought forth one child, the Church has many children to be gathered into one body by the One.

Christ came forth as a bridegroom from his bride's chamber (see Ps 18:6), strong, amiable, terrible, severe and serene. "Remaining in the bosom of his

Father, he took possession of the womb of his mother." Moreover, in this beautiful bridal chamber he united his human and divine natures; the Word made flesh for us leads us to the Father.

Jesus Christ was born of the Virgin Mary and the Holy Spirit.[1] "A virgin conceived without man's cooperation so that she brought forth her child without corruption and she remained a virgin after childbirth." Our Lord Jesus Christ entered his mother's womb and came forth, "preserving intact his mother's body so that he might fill with the honor of maternity and with the holiness of virginity her from whom he deigned to be born."

He chose the virgin whom he would make his mother, "selecting her for his mother, whom he would preserve as a virgin." The Son of God without a mother, the Son of Man without a father, "bringing fertility to his mother on his coming, but not depriving her of integrity on his birth."

We believe in our Lord, Jesus Christ, born of the Holy Spirit and the Virgin Mary, "that blessed Mary, by believing, conceived him whom he, by believing, brought forth." How can this be? By the Holy Spirit and the power of the Most High and the Most Holy One shall be called the Son of God. "Full of faith, Mary conceived Christ in her mind before in her womb." Let it be done, according to your word. "Let him, conceived in a virgin, without man's help, be born of the Holy Spirit and of an inviolate woman, and in him let an unspotted Church be born of the Holy Spirit." "Mary believed, and that which she believed was accomplished in her."

John tells us that all things were made through God's Word.[2] And through his Holy Spirit Mary became pregnant, with Joseph a witness to her virginal chastity. "Though she knew not man, she was found with child by the Holy Spirit" (Mt 1:18). The Holy Spirit wrought the flesh of Christ; and the only begotten Son of God wrought his own flesh. "Wisdom has built himself a house" (Prv 9:1).

How can the Word of God be shut up in Mary's womb? How can he leave heaven? And what would happen to the angels, if he did? "In order that man might eat the bread of angels, the Lord of angels became man."

In conclusion, for Augustine Mary is the paradigm of the Church, virgin and mother. Yet Mary is not greater than the Church, for she is only a member, although a very great member, indeed. As members of the body of Christ, we belong to the childbirth of the virgin mother.

Mary is a perpetual virgin, before, during and after the birth of Christ. Augustine uses the term, mother of God, very little because of the great devotion to Kybele, the Magna Mater of Roman cult. Yet Mary's title would be finally proclaimed at Ephesus (431).

The Church, which imitates mother Mary by procreating her many chil-

---

1. S 215, "At the Recitation of the Creed."
2. S 225, Easter (Nativity).

dren to be gathered into the one body of Christ, we will discuss further in the following chapter.

IV.

THE CHURCH IS A SPIRITUAL MOTHER

(Letter 118)

Augustine has been called the doctor of the Church. For, although he never wrote a treatise on the Church as such, nevertheless, scattered throughout his many works can be found a theology of the Church which would provide a firm foundation for later ecclesiology.

Augustine passed on the traditions of the gospels, Paul and the Fathers, especially Cyprian and Optatus of Milevis. For example, its divine institution, authority, notes or qualities, mission of grace and sacraments.[1]

Types of the Church

For Augustine paradise is an allegory of the Church (see *The City of God* 13, 21).[2] Thus the four rivers of the Garden of Eden are the four gospels, while the saints are represented by green trees bearing their fruitful good works. Whereas the tree of life is Christ the Saint of saints, the tree of the knowledge of good and evil is our own free choice, which spurns the divine will in favor of life's pleasures.

Augustine also compares the Church to Eve, who was formed from Adam's side, symbolizing prophetically the union of Christ and his Church (22, 17). Adam's sleep is a type of Christ's death on the cross, from whom flowed blood and water, that is, the sacraments, which build up the Church. So God made Eve from Adam's rib (see Gn 2:22), and Paul writes of building up the Church, the body of Christ (see Eph 4:12). Therefore, the union of Adam and Eve prefigures the marriage of Christ and the Church. "Adam in the figure of Christ, Eve in the figure of the Church, whence she was called 'the mother of all the living' (Gn 3:20)" (*On the Psalms* 41, 9).

Augustine also describes Noah's ark as a model of the Church (15, 26-27). For even the measurements of the big boat parallel those of Christ's body. And the door in the side of the vessel is similar to the wound in Christ's side.

---

1. See Portalié, *Guide*, 230.
2. Unless otherwise noted, references in this chapter are from *The City of God*.

All the details of the ark's construction symbolize something in the Church. For example, the square timbers are like stable virtues. The incorruptible planks can also refer to the faithful members of the Church (*On John* 6, 19). The Church is where the dove baptizes within and without. So the dove, sent out by Noah, brings back the olive branch which had been baptized by the flood. The three storied ark of the Church contains the descendants of the three sons of Noah. Or the three levels can suggest the three virtues recommended by Paul: faith, hope and charity. Also they can mean the triple harvest of the gospel parable or the three callings within the Church: marriage, widowhood and virginity.

Other types may be used as long as they square with the faith of the city of God. One final allegory. "The nations of the world so filled the Church, and the 'clean' and 'unclean' have been so woven into the texture of the Church's unity in which they are to remain until the final separation" (15, 26).

The prophets also foresaw Christ and his Church (18, 29-37). For example, Isaiah (see 54:1-5). "Your seed shall inherit the Gentiles, and shall inhabit the desolate cities. . . . Your redeemer, the Holy One of Israel, shall be called the God of all the earth."

"The sun has been lifted up and the moon has stood in its order" (Hab 3:10, 11). "Christ ascended into heaven and the Church has been constituted under her king." Habakkuk also predicts the sufferings the Church will undergo.

Daniel (2:34-35) (*On John* 4, 4) saw a stone, cut from a mountain without human hands till it filled the whole earth, signifying the kingdom of the Jews. However, Christians believe that the stone is the Lord born of a virgin.

He is a humble rock, "because not yet had the stone increased and pervaded the whole world. This he showed in his kingdom, which is the Church," with which he filled the earth. However, they only saw a small stone, on which they tripped. Moreover, today some stumble over the mountain which grew from the little rock.

Daniel (7:13-14) (18, 34) speaks of Christ and his Church. "All peoples, tribes and tongues shall serve him—his kingdom shall not be destroyed."

And Haggai (2:7) (18, 35): "I will move all nations; and the desired of all nations shall come." Augustine notes that this prediction is now partially fulfilled. "The rest we may confidently expect by the end of the world." God moved sea and land to make Christ's name known throughout the world. But before the whole world can await and desire Christ's second coming, it must first believe and love him.

Zechariah says (9:9-10) that though the king will come as a poor man, "his power shall be from sea to sea and from the rivers even to the end of the earth."

Malachi (2:5-7) notes that his name will be great among the Gentiles.

"Every place there is a sacrifice and there is offered to my name a clean oblation. For my name is great among the Gentiles, said the Lord of Hosts." So today Christ's priests offer sacrifice from East to West. Was the Jerusalem temple a type of the Church? Augustine responds:

The house of the New Testament is greater than that of the Old because it was built of better materials, namely, those living stones which are human beings renewed by faith and grace. (18, 48)

Yet because Solomon's temple was renovated, it became a prophetic type of the Church.

Haggai comments (2:10): God said, "I will give you peace in that place," that is, where the temple is. And since the restored temple signifies the Church, the true meaning of God's words is: "I will give you peace in that place (the Church) which this place (the rebuilt temple) prefigures." However, not until the house of the New Testament is finally consecrated will its greater glory be seen at the second coming of the Desired of All Nations (see Hag 2:8).

The Master Builder constructs his house, the Church, with the help of his chosen ones, a house without fear of ruin. But until the second coming, the reprobate will live in the house along with the chosen.

However, although the Church may be in a lowly state now, it is preparing for a triumphant life in heaven. Even among Jesus' disciples there was a bad man, whom the Lord tolerated so that his passion would be fulfilled. Thus he teaches us how to deal with evil people in his Church.

When the Holy Spirit came on Pentecost Sunday to give the charism of tongues, this was a sign that the Catholic Church was to be one throughout all the nations (18, 49). Beginning in Jerusalem, the Church expanded outward, preaching the repentance and forgiveness of sins (Acts 1:7-8). Spreading among the Gentiles, the Church thrived, despite many bloody persecutions (18, 50).

Bride of Christ

Like Paul, Augustine calls the Church the Spouse of Christ (S 187). The Son of God was born of a virgin, "so that he might thus link a spotless Church to himself, its spotless Founder" (2 Cor 11:2). The Church imitates the Virgin Mary in mind, though not in body. The Church is both mother and virgin. For Christ made his Church a virgin "by ransoming her from the fornication of demons."

Augustine, speaking to recent converts on the creed (S 213), tells them that they are the Church, including all Christians in this Church, city, region, province, empire and the whole world (see Ps 112), from the rising to the setting sun. "Thus the Catholic Church, our true mother, true bride of her Spouse, exists today."

Finding her a courtesan, Christ made her his virgin bride, signifying their conversion from paganism to their new Lord and Savior. The Church is a virgin in faith. Though Christ has some nuns, virgins in the flesh, "He ought to have all men and women virgins in faith." Paul warns against the deceivers who try to rob the Church of her virginity (see 2 Cor 11:2-4).

But if the Church is a virgin, how can she conceive children? By imitating Mary's virgin birth. "She brings forth Christ because they who are baptized are his members (see 1 Cor 12:27). If, therefore, the Church brings forth members of Christ, she is very much like Mary."

Where is this virgin in the Church? There are different members of the Church, both married and unmarried. "Diverse are these gifts, but all these are one virgin." If his bride is not a virgin in body, at least she is a virgin in mind through her faith, hope and charity. And her Bridegroom feared lest his wife be corrupted by the serpent (*On John* 13, 12).

The Bridegroom owns the whole world, for he purchased it with his blood. And his woven coat of charity signifies the unity of his body, the Church. Moreover, his bride should realize to whom she has vowed her virginity, that is, the King of the Whole World.

Both the indissolubility of marriage and the holiness of the Church as the bride of Christ were linked by the apostle Paul. The difference between the nuptials of the human groom and bride and those of Christ and his Church is this. In the former the bride is different from those who attend the wedding, while in the latter the worthy guests are the brides of Christ.

The Bridegroom sent forth his invitations. "When you know the Bridegroom and the Bride, you may not without reason come to the marriage." Hence every celebration becomes a nuptial. "For the Church's wedding is celebrated." The guests at the King's wedding are indeed the bride. For all the Church is Christ's bride, since, beginning with the incarnation, Christ and his Church became one flesh.

Christ's Church spread to all the nations of the world, the true Catholic Church (S 238). Though we do not see Christ, we do recognize his Church. So we should believe in Christ. The apostles saw Christ, but not his Church, which they, nevertheless, firmly believed in.

> Holding fast to what we see, we shall come to him whom we do not yet see. Thus knowing about the Spouse and his Bride, let us gain more knowledge about them in their marriage records.

Then we will refrain from causing trouble in this holy union.

The division of Christ's garments into four parts at Calvary signifies the fourfold Church, spread to the four winds. However, his seamless coat points to the unity of charity (see Eph 3:29) (*On John* 118, 4).

Mystical Body of Christ

The body of Christ is a favorite Augustinian name for the Church, the internal union of the members of the Church with Christ the head. This is basic Pauline theology, the corporate personality of Christ, which was foreshadowed by the body of Israel, the spouse of Yahweh in the Hebrew Bible.

In the eucharist the members are united in a special way with their head. "We abide in him, when we are his members, and he abides in us when we are his temple." In order to be one of his members we must be joined by the unity of love through the Holy Spirit (*On John* 27, 9). Our soul only quickens the members which are in our body. So a member who is removed from Christ's body is dead. Therefore, there is nothing a member of Christ should fear more than excommunication, through which one is no longer quickened by the Spirit of Christ.

When Jesus hid from his enemies until the proper time, he "indicated that his members would do this, in which members he himself was" (*On John* 28, 1). Christ is wholly in the head and body, so what his members are, he is. However, his members are not necessarily what he is. Jesus told Saul: you are persecuting me in my members (Acts 9:4), whose head I am.

Since we are the body of our Lord Jesus Christ, since we are his members, since we joyfully acknowledge our head, let us say it without hesitation.

Just as the servant does not abide permanently in his master's house, so the servant of sin does not live in the Church forever.

Will Christ, then, remain alone in his house? Will no people remain at his side? Whose head will he be, if there is no body? Or is the Son all this, head and body?

He will remove our sins so that we can stay with him.

Augustine and the other Fathers called the Church "mystical," meaning spiritual or invisible. A body can be a material or spiritual or moral person, so we can say "nobody" or "somebody." Or it can be a political, social or economic corporation.[1] Augustine says that Christ united himself with his Spouse Church into one body, one person. In the Pauline sense, Christ is the head and the Church is his members.

When Christ united himself to humanity in the incarnation, all were raised

---

1. *Corpus* (body) in Roman law can mean a union of persons, a corporation or a moral person. It is synonymous with *collegium*, which can refer to various associations including religious groups. Analagous terms are: *corpus, collegium, universitas, societas, sodalicium*. So, in this sense, the body of Christ could also be the society, college or university of Christ. See A. Berger, *Encyclopedic Dictionary of Roman Law* (Philadelphia: American Philosophical Society, 1953), 416-17, 395 (D 47.22).

up to be one with him as head. So the incarnation is a prerequisite to the foundation of the Church as the body of Christ. Though the head is united with his members, he is of a higher excellence. Just as the limbs of our human body are under the direction of our head, so the members of Christ are subject to him. And as the fullness of our rationality resides in our heads, so the fullness of divinity lies in Christ our head.

Christ animates his body with supernatural life through his head. And the link, joining men and women to him, is his human nature united to his divine nature.[1]

The Church is contiguous with the body of Christ, the whole Christ, one person, bride and groom in one flesh.[2] The Pauline unity of Christ with his Church makes one person, one corporate personality, one moral person as in human marriage. While incorporated into Christ, we enjoy the life of grace (L 187). As we are born of the union of man and woman, so to become a member of the body of Christ, we must be reborn of the union of Christ and his Church (S 121), beginning a new life of grace and justification through baptism. And unless we become a member of the body of Christ, we cannot be saved.

How wide is this body of Christ?[3] In the widest sense, it contains all who attain salvation before and after Christ. In a narrower sense, the body of Christ is the Church on earth. And in the strictest sense it is the visible Catholic Church, although there are varying degrees of participation.

One Dove; Many Tongues

Christ sent his apostles to baptize the nations in the name of the Father, Son and Holy Spirit—to all tongues. "The Holy Spirit signified this by being divided into the tongues united in the dove" (*On John* 6, 10). How better for the Holy Spirit to teach unity than by appearing as a peaceful dove, an innocent, sorrowing bird?

"O Catholic Church, it is to you that it is said: 'my dove is one, the only one of her mother.' " Apart from this dove there is no baptism, for the dove came upon the Lord at his own baptism, communicating to him the power to wash away our sins (13). "It was by this strength, peculiar to himself—that the peace of the Church was secured."

The dove teaches the mystical body from the head of the Lord. "You have baptism, but the charity with which I groan, you have not" (14). Baptism without love profits us nothing. When Christ was baptized, the dove descend-

---

1. S. Grabowski, *The Church, An Introduction to the Study of Saint Augustine* (St. Louis: Herder, 1957), 13; henceforth *The Church.*
2. Grabowski, *The Church,* 19.
3. Grabowski, *The Church,* 69.

ed, which means that when we are baptized we should remain in the unity of charity. "Begin to have charity, begin to have fruit. Let fruit be found within you and the dove will send you within" (19). The Spirit of the Church is the Spirit of Christ. We can never recognize the body of Christ in the eucharist unless we are first members of his body (*On John* 26, 13). "Let them become the body of Christ, if they wish to live by the Spirit of Christ." For no one lives by the Spirit of Christ but the body of Christ.

He who would live, draw near. "Let him be embodied that he may be made to live." So do not shrink from the compact of the members, nor become a rotten member who must be excised, or a deformed member to be spurned by the others. Rather be a fair, fit and sound member, cleaving to the body—for God and by God.

Jesus speaks of his meat and drink, which is "The fellowship of his own body and members, which is the holy Church in his predestined, called, justified and glorified saints and believers."

Though the Lord gave his Paraclete to his Church after his resurrection, the Spirit was manifested many times earlier, for example, to Simeon, Anna and Mary (see Jn 32:6). After he rose from the dead, Jesus breathed on his apostles, giving them the Holy Spirit, as God breathed on Adam in the Garden of Eden.

Then he sent the Advocate on Pentecost with the gift of tongues. Why do we not possess this marvelous charism now? "Because the Church itself now speaks in the tongues of all nations." In the early days since the Church was only in one country, it had to speak in the tongues of all in order to spread the kingdom. Moreover, this wonderful power foretold the universality of the future Church (7).

"Whosoever is not in this Church, does not receive the Holy Spirit." But can we speak in tongues today? "Clearly I do, for every tongue is mine, namely, of the body of which I am a member." The Church, spread over the world, speaks in all languages. And since we are members of that body which talks in all dialects, we also speak in tongues. "For the unity of the members is of one mind by charity, and that unity speaks as one man then spoke."

> We, too, receive the Holy Spirit, if we love the Church, if we are joined together by charity, if we rejoice in the Catholic name and faith . . . As much as everyone loves the Church of Christ, so much has he or she the Holy Spirit. (8)

Paul spoke of the different gifts of the Spirit (1 Cor 12:7-9). "If you love unity, whoever has aught in that unity, has it also for you." So get rid of your envy. The members of the body do not labor only for their own self-interest. Rather the hand protects the eye, while the eye watches out for the hand. Moreover, since all the members are silent, the tongue speaks for them.

"We have the Holy Spirit, if we love the Church. And we love the Church, if we stand firm in its union and charity." "The charity of God is shed abroad in our hearts by the Holy Spirit, which is given to us" (Rom 5:5). Christ did not give the Holy Spirit until he was glorified, "so that he might show in his body the life which we have not now, but which we hope for in the resurrection" (9).

Christ sent the Advocate twice: once on earth for the love of our neighbor and once from heaven for the love of God (*The Trinity* 15, 26). Christ gave the Holy Spirit as God and received the Spirit as man. So he is full of grace and the Holy Spirit (Acts 10:38).

The Paraclete descended on Christ at his baptism, foreshadowing his body, the Church, "in which those who are baptized receive the Holy Spirit in a special manner." However, Jesus came to his baptism, already possessing the Spirit, whom he had since the moment of his incarnation. And before that eternally in heaven.

Just as in the human person there is one vital principle and one body of many members, so in the body of Christ, the Holy Spirit vivifies and coordinates the members.[1] Augustine uses the Pauline and Johannine expression the Spirit of Christ as the unifying and vivifying element of the body of Christ, his Church.[2] The Spirit of Christ is given to the Church, his body, his fullness extended on earth. The Spirit of Christ is the presence of Christ, like the Shekhinah, presence of Yahweh.

Though the Holy Spirit operates in the Church, along with the Father and Son, the animation of the body of Christ is appropriated to the Holy Spirit, who proceeds from the Father and Son. God's Spirit is the uncreated sign of charity and grace. Just as the Spirit is the unifying love of the Father and Son, so also in the body of Christ—unifying and sanctifying his holy Church.

Augustine calls the Church the house of the Trinity, the temple and city of God in heaven and on earth (*Enchiridion* 56). God dwells in his trinitarian Church. "The temple of God, then, that is, of the supreme Trinity, as a whole, is the holy Church, embracing in its full extent, both heaven and earth."

Who are excluded from the body of Christ and its ensoulment, the Holy Spirit? The non-baptized and heretics. Why? Because the Spirit is the unity of the body of Christ as also in the Trinity. So those who rend the body of Christ are incompatible with the Holy Spirit who binds the members of the Church in the unity of charity (*On John* 27:6; L 187).

But cannot the Paraclete, like the Jewish Shekhinah, go where she wishes, even outside the Church? For example, Noah's dove plucked an olive leaf from a tree which was baptized by the flood a far distance from the ark, bringing it home as a sign of peace (see Gn 8:8-11) (*On John* 7, 3).

And cannot the Spirit call those outside the Church to baptism, like Cornelius, who was ordered to go to Peter for instruction and initiation? (Acts

1. Grabowski, *The Church*, 230.
2. See Jn 1:32-33; 15:26; 1 Jn 4:13; Gal 4:6; Rom 8:9-10.

10:1-40). "He was joined to the communion of the Christian people, to whom he was united only by a likeness of good deeds" (*On Baptism Against the Donatists* 1, 8, 10). Cannot faith and a conversion of heart have the same effect as baptism? Augustine's battles against the Donatists and Pelagians prompted him to insist on baptism.

It is true that God can be present in many ways, for example, by his divine omnipresence throughout the world, by his indwelling in the individual soul, by the presence of the Holy Spirit in the body of Christ and by his life in heaven.[1]

Though God is everywhere in the presence of his divinity, he is not everywhere by the grace of his indwelling (L 187). "Therefore, he that is everywhere does not dwell in all, and he does not even dwell equally in those in whom he does dwell." What makes some holier than others except that they have more of the Holy Spirit?

"Those who become wholly unlike him by sinning are said to be far from him. And those who receive his likeness by a virtuous life are said to draw near to him." This is like the human eye, which sees less the farther it is removed from the light. There is, then, a twofold inhabitation of the Holy Spirit: in the individual and in the Church. Though the Christian sinner is cut off from the first, he or she still enjoys the latter presence. However, those who are excommunicated possess neither indwelling.

Marks of the Church

We have seen the Holy Spirit, the inspiration of the unity and the sanctity of the Church. One body, one soul, but many members; one dove and many tongues. The Donatists wanted a super holy Church in which there were no unworthy ministers. However, Augustine answered that it is the holy and sinless Christ who is the real minister of the sacraments.

The sanctity of the Church is founded on the holiness of Christ, whose human nature is sanctified by his divine. The soul of Christ is blessed by the Holy Spirit and Christ, in turn, makes the members of his body holy by his death on the cross. For they are in living union with their head and source of life. Head and body are one Christ. Thus Paul could share the sufferings of Christ (see Col 1:24) (*On John* 108, 5). The members of the Church are holy because they are members of the saintly body of Christ, whom they imitate in their moral actions.

Grabowski notes[2] that the Donatists and the Pelagians contributed to Augustine's theology of the sanctity of the Church. While the Donatists said

---

1. Grabowski, *The Church*, 266.
2. Grabowski, *The Church*, 457.

that the Church was too holy to admit sinners, the Pelagians felt that all Christians should be holy, if they only tried hard enough.

The Donatists, like the Pharisees of old, feared that sinners in the Church might infect the saints by their immoral conduct, while the Pelagians said that the just should be without spot or wrinkle of even venial sins. However, the realistic Augustine taught that such a Church could only be found in heaven. While Pelagius' holiness depended on human effort, Augustine's sanctity is due to God's grace. Moreover, even if the just sin venially, they are still united with Christ.

But why does Christ tolerate evil members in his body? He chose humble fishermen to spread his kingdom (see 1 Cor 1:27-30). "Today both noble and ignoble, learned and unlearned, poor and rich alike draw near to the grace of God" (S 250).

Christ made fishers of fish into fishers of men, telling his disciples to lower their nets to include both the good and bad fish. Also he invited the righteous along with the sinners to his marriage feast (see Mt 22:1-11). So the Church embraces the pious and the impious. Yet it disturbs the good that there are so many evil people in the Church, especially when it seems as if the bad are prospering, even though they may only be enjoying temporalities.

The broken fishing nets of the apostles signify the heresies renting the Church. However, in the post-resurrection account 153 good fish were taken (see Jn 21:12). The earlier fishing expedition shows the Church as it is now, while the post-resurrection story illustrates the future kingdom of heaven. Their boat was almost sinking because of the heavy catch. So when a large number of fish are gathered into the Church in the fourth and fifth centuries, dangers confronted Church discipline and the nets were frayed by schisms and heresies (S 251). The post-resurrection tale in which only good fish were taken anticipates the Church in heaven.

How can sinners be allowed in the Church, the spotless virgin Spouse of Christ? Drunks, fornicators, the concubinous, frauds, astrologers, etc. In the end those who wish to be grain will become bread, while the chaff will be burned. Paul gathered the Gentiles into the Church (S 252), the wheat hidden by the chaff—robbers, slanderers, theatergoers, etc. By their disturbances "they seek in the churches the same things that they do in the theaters," rejecting the spirit while they follow the flesh.

Those who seek earthly rewards in the Church do not understand the temptations, dangers and difficulties promised by God to his Church on earth. However, a rich prize of eternal life and the companionship with the angels awaits these future citizens of heaven (S 252). Moreover, if one so wishes, what was chaff yesterday can become wheat today.

Those 153 good fish that the disciples caught after the resurrection represent the blessed, mystical and great Church. So we can rejoice in the future Church, even though we cannot yet see it. It will be the holy Jerusalem in which there will be no evil ones.

Augustine again asks the question: how can the Lord permit sinners in his Church? He even chose Judas as a disciple (see Jn 51:10). "Why gave he admission to a thief, save to teach his Church to bear patiently with thieves?" Christ gave us a good example by his patience with sinners. While Judas represents the wicked in the Church, Peter, who received the keys, is the leader of the holy Church.

The good really have Jesus Christ always with them through faith, sign, baptism and the eucharist, while the wicked only seem to have Christ by their participation in the Church and sacraments.

Do not be surprised, Augustine warns (S 223), at the large number of bad Christians, who come to the Church, receive communion, praise the fine sermons on morality, etc. For now they are in the Church, but not after the resurrection. The harvest which was sown by the apostles and watered and cared for by the teachers of the Church, is bruised by her enemies. However, in the final winnowing the good grain will be separated from the chaff.

Augustine defends the visibility and unity of the Church, portrayed by the dove (Sg 6:8) (*On John* 6, 6). Christ alone has authority in the Church, though he baptizes through his ministers. But if he gave his authority to his ministers, the unity of baptism would be destroyed.

The true Church of Christ must also be apostolic. To show this Augustine lists the successors of Peter's chair in Rome (L 53). Even if there were some betrayers in the line, still no harm would be done. For Jesus said: do what they say, not what they do (see Mt 23:3). "Thus he made sure that a faithful hope, founded not on man, but on the Lord, should never be scattered by the storm of sacrilegious schism."

What could be worse than to have those who read the apostles' letters in the liturgy be separated from the churches to whom the letters were written. The schismatics scatter their weeds among the grain of the Lord's fields, where they will remain until the final harvest.

Augustine tells Generosus of Constantina (L 53) that his orthodox Christianity is universally taught. So do not let the Donatists tempt you away from the truth. "He is trying to cut you off from the whole and to push you into a part, and to make you a stranger to the promises of God."

No Donatist bishops are found in the Roman lists. Moreover, the individual African churches must be in communion with the universal Church, and in particular with the apostolic see of Rome.

Augustine asks Faustus the Manichaean whether we should believe the apostles who accompanied Jesus Christ and listened to his teaching or some Persian who lived in the fourth century (*Against Faustus* 18, 2). Rather we should put our belief in

a book acknowledged and approved as handed down from the beginning of the Church, founded by Christ and maintained through the apostles and their successors in an unbroken connection all over the world to the present day.

Augustine saw the body of Christ as necessarily catholic, so that local and national churches should agree with the universal Church. Donatist and other heresies were generally local or national in scope. Furthermore, the catholicity of the Church is not only spatial, but also temporal, including all traditions going back to Jesus Christ and after us till the end of time.

Augustine accuses the Donatists of setting up an altar in opposition to the whole world (*On Baptism Against the Donatists* 2, 6, 7). "Why do you not communicate with the churches to which the apostolic epistles have been sent?" Why have you separated yourselves from the truth and the good?

Cyprian chose union with heretics and schismatics, welcoming them into the Church, "holding communion with them when they had been received in the Church without baptism." Rather this, "than be separated from the unity of the Church," and "judging no one, nor depriving anyone of the right of communion if he differ from us."

If Cyprian did not fear to deal with sinners, why should the Donatists separate themselves? "If the Church still existed, the wicked could do no harm to the good in one communion with them." Some reject heretical baptism, while others accept it.

> All of these, catholic unity embraces to her motherly breast, bearing each other's burdens by turns and endeavoring to keep the unity of the spirit in the bond of peace, till God should reveal to one or the other of them any error in their views. (8)

Moreover, if one side has the truth, how can the other side infect them?

Why, then, should the Donatists not break bread with mother Church? Since the Church continues to thrive while including heretics and sinners among its members, "it is clear that it cannot be defiled" (9).

Writing in response to the fundamental letter of Mani, Augustine reminds him that he himself has been a Manichaean in his youth. So what attracted Augustine to the Catholic Church and what kept him there (4)? "The consent of the peoples and nations . . . her authority inaugurated by miracles, nourished by hope, enlarged by love and established by age," the succession of priests from Peter down to the present day episcopate. Also Augustine admires the title "Catholic," which is the universal name of the Church. "Now if the truth is so clearly proved, it must be set before all things that keep me in the Catholic Church."

Augustine was passing on the traditional marks of the Church dating from Irenaeus and the Nicene-Constantinople Creed. For example, against the Donatists he insists on the visibility of the Church as shown in the gospel parables of the light on the candlestick and the city built on a mountain top. Like the woman who touched Jesus' garment (S 62), "the faith of the few 'touches' the body of Christ, while the throng of the many presses in on him. " If we are his body, what he felt in the midst of the crushing crowd, that the Church suffers now. Though it is pressed by many, it is touched by few. While the flesh pushes roughly against it, faith caresses it gently. Lift up your eyes of faith to see the body of Christ, the Church; touch the border of Christ's garment, and receive saving health.

How is the visible, hierarchical and social Church related to the mystical body of Christ? The body of Christ is the Church, "not this church or that, but diffused over all the world." Furthermore, it includes not only the living, but also our ancestors and our descendants. For all members of the Church are members of his body, with Christ as their head (*On the Psalms* 56).

Augustine warns about those who are only bodily in the Church. "The whole ought to be within. If that which man sees is within, why is that which God sees without?" (S 62).

The City of God

How is the Church related to the city of God (*On the Psalms* 99, 4)? Zion is the city of God. "What is the city of God, but the holy Church? For men who love one another and who love God who dwells in them constitute a city unto God," a city based on the law of love. Moreover, this love is God (see 1 Jn 4:8). So if we are full of love, we are full of God. "And many, full of love, constitute a city full of God," called Zion.

Gilson writes[1] that those who seek earthly peace constitute the city of man, while those who pursue heavenly rest are in the city of God. However, he adds that the city of God, which includes all who are predestined to eternal life, cannot be contiguous with the Catholic Church, for it includes those predestined for heaven, who are not yet members of the Church, for example, Saul before his conversion.

However, Gilson sees the Church as the visible incarnation of the city of God. As in the gospel parables, the city of God and the city of man are intermeshed until the final judgment. Some who are outside the Church now, will join later, while some who are members of the Church at the present moment, may leave it.[2] This is why Augustine went to such great lengths to bring back the wanderers. For those who live in the Church in a bond of love are reigning with Christ in his kingdom.

The kingdom of God, or the city of God is spiritual so its boundaries are not visible. Those who believe in Christ the King—there is his kingdom, one

---

1. E. Gilson, *The Christian Philosophy of St. Augustine* (New York: Random House, 1960), p. lxiii; henceforth *Christian Philosophy*.

2. *The City of God* 1, 35. Unless otherwise noted, citations in this section are from here.

will, one love. Unity of doctrine distinguishes the city of God from the city of man, where diverse opinions are not only tolerated, but even encouraged. Gilson comments[1] "The Church, the living incarnation of the city of God, did nothing more than maintain the tradition of the Jewish people whose heir she was and whose doctrine she enriched." Because of her universality, the Church had to preserve unity of doctrine. "The city of God, whose existence is bound to the unity of the faith, cannot allow its teachers the right to attack and contradict her." The result would be a city of confusion.

However, God can draw some good out of the attacks of heretics, for the Church suffers along with Christ. Moreover, intellectual arguments bring forth her wisdom. And she is kind and forgiving to her enemies. Also God allows persecution for the Church's own good, lest she grow complacent (18, 51).

Since the city of God is not of this world, it sometimes shows intolerance toward mundane things.[2] And since the Divine Metropolis feels an obligation to reform the city of man, an inevitable conflict arises between the two cities. Is a reconciliation possible? In the earthly realm, temporal goods help ensure earthly security, while in the heavenly city they are used toward eternal peace (19, 14).

How does the city of God operate in the home? Domestic peace relies on the "harmonious interplay of authority and obedience among those who live there." A religious family lives by faith, yet they are all wayfarers on the road to the heavenly city. "Those who command serve those they rule not out of lust for power, but out of duty, not out of pride, but rather from solicitude."

Gilson[3] calls Augustine a theologian of history, interpreted in the light of revelation through Wisdom, Christ.

Can the earthly city of man be connected to the city of God? Why could not the Church bring about a human unity and peace in the love of Christ? "It was enough that the city of God exist in order to inspire men with the desire to organize the earth into a single society made to the image and likeness of the heavenly city." Could not there be a third city of temporal justice between the city of truth and the city of error?

"To his successors Augustine bequeathed the ideal of a society whose bond of union is the divine Wisdom. The Emperor Charles (ninth century) dreamed of an empire embodying the city of God. Later emperors either aided or fought the Church, but their temporal realms disappeared. The Church, on the other hand, will remain as long as the earthly history of the city of God endures.

"The city capable of embracing all men is the city of God, that is, the Church." It lives by faith, seeking a heavenly rather than an earthly peace.

1. Gilson, *Christian Philosophy*, pp. lxix-lxx.
2. Gilson, *Christian Philosophy*, p. lxxi.
3. Gilson, *Christian Philosophy*, pp. lxxvi-lxxix.

But the Church can make use of temporal order till eternal life is reached (19, 17).

> So long as the heavenly city is wayfaring on earth, she invites citizens from all nations and all tongues and unites them into a single pilgrim band. She takes no issue with that diversity of customs, laws and traditions whereby human peace is sought and maintained. Instead of nullifying or tearing down, she preserves and appropriates whatever in the divers races is aimed at one and the same objective of human peace, provided only that they do not stand in the way of the faith and worship of the one, supreme and true God. (19, 17)

The unity of the city of God is based on the one God. On the other hand, pagans, having a multiplicity of deities, are divided in their beliefs. The heavenly city on earth invites all nations to join, asking only that they believe in the one true God, seeking "the perfectly ordered and harmonious communion of those who find their joy in God and in one another in God." Thus we see that the central message of Augustine's *The City of God* is that human unity is impossible without one God and one Church.

The unity of the Church is based on the Triunity of God (*Enchiridion* 15-16). "The Church should follow after the Trinity, as a house after its dweller, a temple after its god and a city after its founder." The whole Church, here and hereafter is one fellowship in eternity, but now united in charity. "The temple of God, of the supreme Trinity as a whole, is the holy Church, that is, the Church universal in heaven and earth." While the Church of heaven will be known when we join it, the pilgrim Church on earth is better known when we belong to it and so are redeemed by Christ.

The trinitarian image was preserved in the hierarchy of the early Church where the bishop represented the Father, the deacon the Son and the deaconess the Holy Spirit.

In this chapter we have seen some of Augustine's views of the Church. His ecclesiology was at least partially conceived in reaction to certain heresies such as the Donatists and the Pelagians. Augustine is a realist, holding that the Church, although the body and spouse of Christ, still contains its share of sinners. It is one, holy, catholic and apostolic under the guidance of the invisible Good Shepherd, who has delegated his care to his visible shepherds.

Having seen Augustine's theology of the Church, let us next examine her authority.

V.

THE FRIENDLY SHADE OF AUTHORITY

(The Morals of the Catholic Church 7)

Roman Authority

Before seeing Augustine's view of authority, it might be profitable to explore the Roman background. To most people authority (*auctoritas*) means power, threatening and overbearing. However, this is far from its original meaning. More fundamentally, authority is a moral or social influence, leaning more toward good example than sanctions and punishments.

Auctoritas (and *auctor*) come from the Latin verb, *augeo*, which means to cause one to grow and flourish, to enrich or to supply what is wanting. "When one increased (*augebat*) what another had, so as to fill up a deficiency, this increasing or filling up was called '*auctoritas*.' " For example, a teacher helping his student or a tutor his ward.[1]

There seem to be parallels to *aedificare* (*oikodomein*), a building up of persons and institutions, in the Pauline sense,[2] just the opposite of tearing down, belittling, etc.

Authority can be used of persons or groups that are given their due in respect and obedience. For example, the people of Rome (*populi*), the emperor (*auctoritas principis*), officials, parents, Roman law codes, etc.[3]

In private law a tutor or auctor shows *auctoritas* when he acts for his ward (*pupillus*). Authority can also be a guarantee on the part of a vendor.

The concept of the emperor's authority (*auctoritas principis*) appears with Augustus when he transferred the *res publica* to the senate and the people when he was named "Augustus" in January, 27, B.C. Augustus notes in his autobiography, "Though I was superior to others in authority, I had no more power than my colleagues in the magistracy." Here Augustus is referring to his personal authority, his moral and social influence. On the other hand, power (*potestas*) means legal force.

Berger (369) sees the emperor's authority as "personal prestige, the authority, the high esteem, which the emperor enjoyed as the first citizen of

---

1. Introduction to *Sandars' Institutes of Justinian* (Chicago: Callaghan, 1876), 30.
2. See 1 Cor 14:4; 1 Thes 5:11; 1 Cor 8:10; 1 Cor 14:17, 1 Cor 8:1.
3. See Berger, *Encyclopedic Dictionary*, 368-69.

Rome." All his acts and orders are important. The senate and the jurists also used imperial authority. In time the *auctoritas principis* became sovereign especially in the fourth and fifth centuries.

Cassiciacum Dialogues

Augustine developed his theology of authority during the summer of 386 at his friend Verecundus' villa at Cassiciacum outside of Milan with the companionship of his mother Monica, his friend Alypius, his brother Navigius, his son Adeodatus along with two cousins and two pupils.

While he and Adeodatus awaited baptism, they mulled over philosophical questions such as the meaning of happiness and what part authority played in their conversion.

Writing against the Academics (386) (F), Augustine notes that both reason and authority are equally sources of knowledge. However, reason alone is not sufficient. So Augustine leans on divine authority. This is the basic meaning of authority, as we have seen, namely, a supplying of a want or need in his weak understanding.

Anyone who is still searching for the truth is imperfect, remarks Augustine's friend Trygetius. However, philosophy's promise of liberty tempts one to throw off the yoke of authority (1, 1-9). Licentius adds that unless we reach truth, we are imperfect. For God alone knows truth.

Augustine addresses the seeming dichotomy of reason and authority. "We are impelled toward knowledge by a twofold source: the force of authority and the force of reason. And I am resolved never to deviate in the least from the authority of Christ for I find none more powerful" (3, 20-43). Augustine is determined to grasp truth not only by faith, but also by comprehension. Thus he hopes that Platonism and scripture will not contradict each other.

Speaking on order (386) (F), Augustine notes

> that when the obscurity of things perplexes us, we follow a twofold path: reason, or at least, authority. Philosophy sends forth reason and it frees scarcely a few.

It helps us understand the mysteries as far as possible. True philosophy teaches us the eternal First Principle, the Trinity, incarnation, etc. (1, 4-15).

In acquiring knowledge, "we are of necessity led in a twofold manner: by authority and by reason" (1, 9-26). Timewise authority is first, while "in the order of reality, reason is prior." Augustine adds that while authority is a safe guide for the uninstructed, "Reason is better adapted for the educated."

Moreover, for those who "seek to learn great and hidden truths, authority alone opens the door." Then one enters to live a perfect life, becomes docile, and, among other things, one sees "what reason itself is, which one—now strong and capable after the cradle of authority—follows and comprehends."

Some just meekly follow authority, applying themselves to right living, while bypassing the arts. Though Augustine feels that these may be unhappy here on earth, they will be swiftly liberated in the next life.

Although authority is partly divine and partly human, "the true, solid and sovereign authority is that which is called divine." For our human senses can be fooled. On the other hand, divine authority not only exceeds human power, but also "in the very act of leading us onward, shows us" how God debased himself for our sake, encouraging us to soar up to our intellect from our senses (1, 9-27).

Though human authority can deceive, it is better "in those who propose various proofs for their teachings, insofar as the mind of the unlearned can grasp them" and live accordingly.

In his discussion on the immortality of the soul (387) (7, 12) (F) Augustine comments:

> To trust the word of another is one thing; to trust our own reason is a different thing. To take something on authority is a great timesaver and involves no toil.

Read of great men who guide the unlearned, those who were too preoccupied and so "could find no other safe road to truth." For if they trust too much to reason, they may be misled.

"It is a decided advantage to trust a most reliable authority and to shape our conduct according to it." Augustine applauds this way for his friend Evodius. However, if he pursues the path of reason, he has a long difficult road ahead to arrive at a state free from false arguments.

Augustine, Apologist

Augustine seeks to show the Manichees that the authority of Christ and his Church is superior to that of Mani and his disciples. For example, in his *Morals of the Catholic Church* (388) (7, 11) (N), Augustine lauds the wisdom and authority of scripture.

> So when we are hastening to retire into darkness, it will be well that by the appointment of adorable wisdom we should be met by the friendly shade of authority, and should be attracted by the wonderful character of its contents, and by the utterances of its pages, which, like shadows, typify and attemper the truth.

What more could God have done for our salvation? Once again we find the root meaning of authority, namely, a supplying of what is lacking in our weak human nature by God's grace through his holy Church and scripture.

However, Mani does not believe that there is wisdom in the Catholic Church (*Against the Letter of Mani* 4) (397) (N).[1] Augustine replies that there are many other things that keep him in the bosom of holy mother Church. For example:

> the consent of peoples and nations keeps me in the Church; so does her authority inaugurated by miracles, nourished by hope, enlarged by love, established by age.

None of these things does Augustine find among the Manichees.

Furthermore, though Mani claims to be an apostle of Christ, Augustine can find no evidence of this in scripture. "For my part I should not believe the gospel except as moved by the authority of the Catholic Church" (5). Moreover, "when those on whose authority I have consented to believe in the gospel tell me not to believe in Mani, how can I not consent?"

Furthermore, if the gospels verify Mani's claim, "you will weaken my regard for the authority of the Catholics, who bid me not to believe in you." For it was through the Catholics that Augustine received his faith in the gospels and the Acts of the Apostles, "since both writings alike Catholic authority commends to me."

Later Augustine replies to Faustus the Manichaean and his false interpretation of scripture (400) (32, 19) (N). "Your design is clearly to deprive scripture of all authority, and to make everyone's mind the judge of what passage one approves or disapproves of. Thus the reader would make scripture subject to him or herself."

So "instead of asking the high authority of scripture the reason of approval, every one makes personal approval the reason for thinking a passage correct." Moreover, if you set aside authority, to which poor soul do you turn? "Set aside authority and let us hear the reason for your beliefs."

Yet Faustus does not hesitate to lean on the strange authority and opinions of Mani. For example, that Atlas holds up the earth. He believes this and other absurd things without proof.

> Why not rather submit to the authority of the gospel, which is well founded, so confirmed and so generally acknowledged and admired, and which has an unbroken series of testimonies from the apostles down to our own day.

Thus there is more truth in the incarnation of the Son of God who suffered for us than in the Manichaean belief that God suffers the corruption of human nature and so merits punishment. When we compare the authority of Mani with that of the apostles, we find that though both writings are genuine, Mani preaches the gospel of the devil, while the apostles teach the gospel of Christ. And he who spreads another gospel is cursed (see Mt 8:11).

---

1. Next few quotes are from here.

Pastoral Concern

Shortly after his ordination in Hippo, Augustine writes to his Manichaean friend Honoratus on the value of believing (391-92) (F),[1] pointing out some of the errors of the Manichees. Augustine also wants to vindicate the proper authority in religious truth and to demonstrate the priority of faith over reason. As a young man Augustine had tried the Manichees and the Academics in his long search for God, believing that the human mind is agile enough to perceive the truth if it can find the way, which would have to be shown by some divine authority. But "it remained to find out what that authority was." For many claimed to have God's approval. Thus Augustine encountered a forest of different opinions.

He suggests to Honoratus that if he wants to stop his suffering, he should follow the path of Catholic teaching passed down by the apostles.

> Unless those things are believed which later, if he has succeeded and been worthy, each one attains to and perceives, and without a certain weighty power of authority, true religion cannot at all be rightly entered into. (9, 21)

"What we understand, accordingly, we owe to reason; what we believe, to authority; and what we have an opinion of, we owe to error." Anyone who understands believes, and one who has an opinion believes also. However, not all who believe or opine, understand.

There are different types of people. For example, the blessed who believe the truth itself; and then there are those who seek after and love the truth which they believe on authority. Moreover, there is a great difference between thinking that we know something and "believing under the influence of some great authority, what we realize we do not know." If we follow the latter course we will avoid severe errors of inhumanity and pride. Once again, Augustine sees authority filling a gap in our knowledge (*augere*), helping our knowledge to grow through authority and faith.

We believe what we do not yet know. This is found in children in relation to the authority of their parents. For it is the duty of the mother and father to fill up the wants in their children's lives, to help them grow (*augere*), physically, intellectually and morally.

But how do the children know that these two grownups are their real parents? Certainly not through reason. Their parenthood is believed by the father on the authority of the mother. And mother gets her assurance of her offspring from her midwife, nurse or other attendants at the birth of her child (12, 26). "Yet we believe here what we admit that we cannot know." Moreover, on this familial faith is built the firm foundation of human society.

Augustine feels that it is healthy to believe before we use our reason. "And

---

1. Next few quotes are from *The Advantage of Believing*.

with faith itself to prepare the ground to receive the seeds of truth." For this is the way to safety for sick souls. Thus Augustine himself believed in Christ without resorting to reason.

> I have believed no one except the affirmed opinion and the wide-spread report of peoples and nations and that the mysteries of the Catholic Church have everywhere taken possession of those peoples.

Why not seek Christ's teachings from these believers, since "it was under the influence of their authority that I already believed that Christ had taught something profitable?" For example, Victorinus, Ambrose and Monica.

> I believed a report which had the strength of numbers, agreement and antiquity, while the Manichees are few, confused, novel and offer nothing that has the dignity of authority. (14, 31)

Augustine learns about Christ "from those whom my faith in him had come." Moreover, he reminds Honoratus that if he wishes to find happiness, he should be willing to obey the Lord's precepts, "the commands which he willed to strengthen by such weighty authority as that of the Catholic Church" (15, 33).

Since it is not easy to find God's truth, we should imitate the wise. Moreover, God provides miracles to help our belief, "so that our lives and habits might be purged and thus become amenable to the acceptance of reason." What better way than that the Wisdom of God became human, showing us how divine mercy extends to our weakness.

> This is the healthiest authority (16, 34). This is the first way of lifting our souls from their dwelling on earth. This is the conversion to the true God from the love of this world.

Authority alone can make the foolish wise.

> We must not give up hope that God has established some authority, on which, if we rely, just as on a sure step we will be raised up to God . . . This authority moves us in two ways, by miracles and by the crowds who follow it.

But these things are not necessary for the wise, while they are difficult for a sinful soul and one who cannot see the truth. "Authority is at hand to make us fit for this and to allow us to purge ourselves."

So authority prevails, partly through miracles and partly through the crowds of believers. Through miracles "divine authority turned wandering souls to itself." But why are there no miracles today? How about the heavens, seasons, spring time, birth and growth? We become jaded and even bored with these daily wonders of God.

The miracles of Christ were wrought so that the divine authority might move the crowds and so spread the kingdom of God on earth. Moreover, heroic Christian lives of the saints and martyrs continue to influence us. For when we see this progress and fruit, "can we hesitate to bury ourselves in the bosom of that Church?"

> Starting from the apostolic chair down through successions of bishops, even unto the open confession of all mankind, it has possessed the crown of authority. (17, 35)

In his *Confessions*[1] Augustine also traces his journey toward the truth, guided by the authority of the Church and scripture. The Church asks us to believe in many mysteries that cannot be demonstrated. Yet Augustine began to see that he believed many things without seeing them. For example, his faith in history, friends, physicians, parents, all constituting a sound basis for a sane life.

The Lord persuades Augustine to hear "those who believe in your books, which you have established as authoritative among nearly all peoples" (6, 5-7).

Augustine feels that he is too weak to discover the truth by his reason alone.

> We had need of the authority of holy scripture. I had already started to believe that you would never have granted such high authority throughout every land to that scripture, unless you had willed that we believe in you through it and that we seek you through it. (6, 5-8)

The authority of scripture is worthy of belief because "while readily available to be studied by all, it yet kept the grandeur of its mystery under a more profound sense." So although scripture is open to all, the difficult passages are clear only to the few, "but to many more than if it failed to reach such a height of authority, or if it failed to draw such crowds of people into the lap of its holy humility."

What is important is that "the crest of the authority of the Christian faith is spread so high throughout the whole world." For all of these divine marvels would not have been done for us by God unless there were a life beyond the grave.

Despite Augustine's many temptations, God took care of him. And he still believes in God and his divine providence.

> And that in Christ, your Son, Our Lord, and in your holy scripture, which the authority of the Catholic Church guarantees, you have established the way of human salvation into that life which will come after death. (7, 7-11)

Here we see *auctoritas* in a more legal sense as a guarantee of the genuinity and value of scripture. Moreover, these sacred writings overcome all false

---

1. Next few quotes are from the *Confessions* (397-401) (F).

teachings "by their eminent authority throughout the whole world" (12, 26-36).

Augustine sees in scripture "a firmament of authority" stretched like a protecting skin overhead. "Indeed, your divine scripture is of even more authority now that those mortals through whom you gave us the sacred writings have died" (13, 15-16).

As God covered sinful Adam and Eve with protecting skins, "so you have stretched out the firmament of your book like a skin," given to us by the mortals when they died. Moreover, "the powerful establishment of authority in your writings put out by them is sublimely extended over all things subject to them today."

Augustine contrasts and links authority and obedience (13, 23-33). For the Church includes both those in spiritual authority and the spiritual subjects of authority. "Spiritual persons, whether they hold positions of authority or obedience, judge in a spiritual way."

Augustine notes in his *The City of God* (10, 32),[1] that human weakness should always submit to divine authority, like the angels who are our superiors.

The philosopher Porphyry himself was dissatisfied in his search for a universal way to salvation. "He still felt that he needed a supreme authority which should be followed in this important matter" (10, 32).

Authority and obedience begin in the home (see 1 Tim 5:8). "Those who have the care of others give the orders, while those who are cared for must obey" (19, 14). Once again, authority is concerned with care for those in need, a supplying of wants, a helping to grow.

However, Augustine points out that in the heavenly city those who command serve those under them rather than dominating them with their power. This is compatible with the basic meaning of *augere* and *auctoritas*, as we have seen.

Furthermore, the ordered harmony between authority and obedience in the home has a relationship with that of the city, of which the family is a microcosm (19, 16).

Moreover, while the earthly city seeks peace and harmony of authority and obedience among its citizens, the heavenly metropolis uses earthly peace here below where there is common cause concerning human life.

Thus Augustine tells his flock that they must obey civil authorities (see Rom 13:1-3) (S 13, 6) (410) (W). Paul reminds us that all authority comes from God. And if we act justly, just authority will praise us. Or if unjust authority condemns our just works, God will reward us. For example, the martyr Cyprian praised the civil authorities who condemned him.

Augustine also addresses civil magistrates. "All you who wish to exercise authority over others, be instructed how not to judge crookedly and so lose

---

1. Next few quotes are from *The City of God* (413-26).

your own soul even before you destroy anyone else's flesh." Some get their office on merit, while others buy it. Judge yourself before judging others. Job praises God's authority even in the midst of his misfortunes.

Notice Job's understanding of God's absolutely all-dominating authority and power. . . . It is wholly with God that all power and authority and supreme power and authority lie.

Thus God has control over Satan (S 15A, 6) (W) (410).

The gospel story tells us of the Centurion, who though he was a man of authority, was also under a higher authority. Moreover, Jesus, the ultimate authority, preached his kingdom also to the Gentiles (see Mt 8:8) (S 62, 4) (W) (399, 407/8).

Augustine does not teach contempt for civil authority. Since all authority is from God, whoever opposes authority, opposes God (see Rom 13:1-2). But what if authority orders us to do something evil? "Make light of authority by respecting it." In human affairs we obey orders unless they are against the law. However, "we do not show contempt for authority when we decide to be of service to a higher one." Hence a lower authority should not be chagrined if we obey the higher. For example, if the emperor commands one thing and the governor another, we obey the first (*auctoritas principis*). And so we obey God also over civil authority.

Conclusion

The authority of God, Christ, Church and scripture fills up a need in our weak souls, increasing our knowledge of God, helping us to grow spiritually (*augere*), saving us from our sins (*servare*). Moreover, this is freely given (*gratis*).

God and his Son are the authors and guarantors of the Church and scripture. They take care of and protect us like a tutor or a parent, while building us up and helping us to grow.

In the following chapter we will see the authority of the Church as expressed in her ministry, which should be nurturing rather than dominating.

VI.

NOT AT THE HEAD, BUT AT THE SIDE

(*The City of God* 19, 29)

Hierarchical Church

Church officers in Augustine's time were often chosen by the people, for example, Ambrose at Milan and Augustine at Hippo. Grabowski[1] remarks that Augustine uses the term *ordo* to signify clerical ranks. For order is necessary for peace in the human body and in social corporations such as the family, city or the body of Christ. "Peace is—the calm that comes of order. And order is an arrangement of like and unlike things whereby each of them is disposed in its proper place" (*The City of God* 19, 13).[2]

But how about the priesthood of the laity? Truly there is one priest, Jesus Christ, and his body is an extension of this priesthood. So all Christians are priests insofar as they partake of the one priesthood of their head (20, 13). John writes that they will be priests of God, reigning with him for a thousand years (see Rev 20:7). John is speaking not only of bishops and presbyters, but of all Christians, because they are members of his body. So "we call them all priests insofar as they are members of one priest, a chosen race, a royal priesthood (see 1 Pt 2:9). For Christ is a priest forever according to the order of Melchizedek.

As priests, we offer our bodies in a sacrifice of spiritual service (see Rom 21:1). And our soul also gives itself to God (10, 6). Furthermore, when the whole congregation is offered as a sacrifice to God by the high priest, it is at the same time mediator, priest and sacrifice. Thus the Church, herself, the body of Christ, is offered as an oblation on the altar.

Ordination to holy orders, like baptism, can be received only once, because it leaves an indelible mark on the soul of the recipient, thus heretical or apostate priests are still clerics.

Augustine applies lots (*cleri*) to those in orders (*On the Psalms* 68, 16-17). "Lots according to the promise of God are called those parts of the inheritance which were distributed to the people" (Nm 18:20). However, the Levites did not receive lots since they were sustained by tithes.

---

1. Grabowski, *The Church*, 95.
2. Unless otherwise noted, quotes in this section are from *The City of God*.

Christian ministers are called clerics because Matthias, chosen by lot, was the first shepherd ordained by the apostles (Acts 1:26). *Cleri* can also mean the lots of inheritance, which in the New Testament is everlasting life. As we have seen, clerics were often chosen by the people in Augustine's time to build up the body of Christ, converting, instructing, baptizing, caring, presiding, preaching, blessing, witnessing, reconciling, etc.

Augustine uses the term *praepositus* of the minister who presides over the Christian community, administering the sacraments and the word of God. He can be a bishop, presbyter, deacon or of a lower order.

Qualifications? In order to be chosen a minister of the Church one should be free of crime. So when Paul called for the ordination of bishops, elders or deacons, he did not demand impeccability, but rather that there be no crime: murder, adultery, fornication, theft, fraud, etc. (*On John* 41, 10). Actually the requirements for the clergy did not differ widely from the qualities demanded of Roman officials.[1]

Ordained deacons, who are the bishop's right-hand men, catechize, distribute the eucharist and do social work, while the presbyters are delegated by the bishop to administer the sacraments and preach.

However, we should never forget that it is the Lord who builds up his house, the Church (*On the Psalms* 126, 1). Otherwise the ministers work in vain, that is, those "who preach the word of God in the Church, the ministers of God's mysteries." Though we are laboring now, others have prepared the foundations before us. While the minister speaks to our ears externally, the

---

1. See J. Mohler, *The Origin and Evolution of the Priesthood* (New York: Alba House, 1970), chap. 2. For good insights into fifth century clergy see the *Shirmondian Constitutions*, title 10:

    The faithful recommendation of a religious priest demands a discipline that is commendable to the world. For in accordance with good morals he insists that clerics who serve the sacred ministries shall not be joined to extraneous women whom they excuse by the disgraceful association of the appellation of "sister." For we trust that there is such reverence for God in consecrated minds that the consciousness of a wicked persuasion does not know the habitation of this licentious retreat. But though such wicked persuasion may not enter into such an association and friendship, rumor contaminates and the addition of the opposite sex gives an opportunity for evil morals, since the example of obscene suspicion entices to the allurements of crime those persons situated outside and living according to the law.

    Since these things are so, Your Illustrious and Excellent Magnificence by posting edicts everywhere shall publish the sanction of the present imperial oracle, so that if any person relies upon any rank whatever in the priesthood or is distinguished by the honor of the clergy, he shall know that consorting with extraneous women is forbidden him. This concession alone is granted to him, that he may have within the bounds of his own home his mother, daughters and sisters german; for in connection with these, the natural bond permits no perverse crime to be considered. Chaste affection, however, demands that those women who lawfully obtained marriage before their husbands assumed the priesthood should not be deserted. For these women have made their husbands worthy of the priesthood by their association are not unsuitably joined to clerics (Theodosius 5, 8) (420) (*Theodosian Code, Novels and Sirmondian Constitutions*, tr. C. Pharr (Princeton University Press, 1952), 481-82.

Lord builds us up within, where he admonishes, teaches and strengthens our faith.

The house of God, the people of God, the temple of God, Jerusalem, is the Church, which Christ guards while the bishops administer. "For a higher place was for this reason given to the bishops to superintend and guard the people as a vinedresser oversees his vineyard."

A bishop can just do so much for his people, since he usually sees them only at the liturgy, if then. He certainly cannot peer into the secret corners of their hearts or go around looking through their windows to see what they are doing. So unless the Lord keeps the city, the watchman wakes in vain. For he keeps guard while we are awake or asleep.

"We guard you in our office of stewards, but we wish to be guarded together with you." Augustine is not only their *praepositus* and teacher, but also a fellow Christian and fellow student of the Master.

Being a bishop means work: caring, guiding, teaching, ministering, admonishing, etc. Moreover, the labor far exceeds the dignity of the job. "Thus no man can be a good bishop, if he loves his title more than his task" *(praeesse dilexit, non prodesse)* (19, 19).

Bishops in synod govern their province or region under the guidance of the apostolic see in Rome. Peter was designated the head of the Church by Christ who called him a rock because he signified the Church (S 76). Christ is the rock and Peter the Christian people. "Upon myself, the Son of the living God, I will build my Church."

Peter is both strong and weak, because the Church of Christ has both strong and weak members. Christ told Peter to feed his lambs and sheep (see Jn 21:15) (S 147). "Peter prefigured the unity of all pastors, of good pastors, who know that they feed Christ's sheep for Christ and not for themselves." Christ gave the keys to Peter, who represents the universality and unity of the Church (S 295).

We have already discussed the successors to Peter in the Roman church, whose continuity showed the catholicity in time which prompted Augustine's conversion.[1] Rome occupies a special place among the apostolic sees. So Augustine venerates the list of Peter's heirs.

Thus Secundus, bishop of Carthage, was able to ignore a heretical conspiracy, "when he saw that he was united by pastoral letters to the church of Rome, where the primacy of the apostolic chair has always flourished and to those countries from which the gospel came to Africa" (L 43). African councils, for example, opposing the Pelagians, sent their proceedings to Rome, which, in turn, mailed a rescript to the bishops of the Church condemning Pelagius' teachings.

In his letter to Generosus (L 53) Augustine notes that in the list of the apostolic successors of Peter in Rome no Donatist bishops are named.

---

1. *Against the Fundamental Letter of Mani* 4; *Against Faustus* 28, 2.

Moreover, even if a betrayer had been included, there would still be no harm done to the Church (see Mt 23:3), since our hope is based not on human leaders, but on the Lord. So the Church cannot be scattered by schisms.

Elsewhere Augustine compares the Church tradition to a stream of water (*On the Psalms* 45, 7). "These rivers flowed out of the bosom of Paul, Peter, John and the other apostles and other faithful evangelists. Since these rivers flowed from one source, many streams of the river make glad the city of God."

The twofold task of the Christian minister: to preach the word of God and minister the mysteries. The Lord himself gave us his sacraments (L 54): baptism in the name of the Trinity, the communion of his body and blood, "and whatever else is commanded in the canonical writings." Other observances come down to us through tradition. "We understand that they have been ordained or recommended to be kept by the apostles themselves, or by plenary councils." For example, the feasts of the passion, resurrection and pentecost, "and other such observances as are kept by the universal Church wherever it is found." As to other customs—follow the traditions of the local churches.

A frequent problem. Should the clergy flee the attacks of barbarians and heretics, or should they stay with their flocks? The people are distraught and anxious without the celebration of the mysteries. However, when the priests remain on duty, insofar as the Lord gives them strength, baptism, reconciliation and communion comfort, edify and encourage the people.

> What a blessing it is for Christian people not to be deprived of the presence of Christ's priests in the midst of present dangers. You see, too, the evil effects of their absence, when they seek the things that are their own, not the things that are Jesus Christ's (see Phil 2:21).

For Jesus Christ did not flee his enemies, but rather laid down his life for others. Furthermore, flight in times of persecution on the part of the shepherds can give bad example to their flocks. However, it would not be appropriate that all the priests be killed so that none were left for the future.

The life of a bishop leaves little time for himself, observed Augustine of his mentor, Ambrose (see *Confessions* 6, 3). Though Augustine admired the honors the people of Milan bestowed on their pastor, his practice of priestly celibacy seemed too difficult. Moreover, when Augustine tried to approach Ambrose for spiritual advice, he was cut off by "crowds of busy men, to whose troubles he was a slave," so that he had little time for eating or reading.

The Lord wants his clerics to look forward to death with fortitude, even desiring it and in the meantime "to undertake the labor of their administration without anxiety" (L 10). However, those who seek church office for the honor and like the hustle and bustle of the daily activity, do not want death to cut short their spans.

The house of God is a city with builders and sentries (see Gal 4:10-11).

Paul guarded his churches. "He kept watch to the utmost of his power over those over whom he was set. The bishops also do this. For a higher place was for this reason given to the bishops, that they might be themselves the superintendents, and, as it were, the guardians of the people." After all, that is what *episcopus* means (*On the Psalms* 126).

The bishop has a perilously high station and one that demands humility, for Augustine knows that the Lord is the true keeper of his flock. Love must be the motivational force behind a bishop's service to his people (L 110), so he is never too busy to lend a helping hand to those in need.

The bishop should be a good shepherd, serving his church with fear and not for the purpose of personal gain (S 46) (see Ez 34:1-16). Bishops are Christians for themselves and leaders for others. The Good Shepherd will help them speak the truth. When mouthing their own ideas, the bishops are only feeding themselves. However, if they speak the Lord's words, the Lord himself nourishes the faithful.

Many Christians come to Christ by an easier road because they carry a smaller burden. Bishops, however, bear a heavier load. So Augustine asks for the prayers of his congregation. For when bishops come to judgment, they will be measured on how well they ministered to their churches.

Augustine always has "the best interests of those whom we shepherds have to feed in Christ" (L 60). So he believes that it is better not to pick as ministers servants of God who are looking for an easier life outside of their monasteries. For they often become worse, once they are away from the strict regime of the cloister.

Inside the monastery only the best are chosen for ordination. Moreover, it is unfair to the regular clergy to ordain just any ex-monk who happens to come along. For even if a monk is good and observes celibacy, he may still lack the education and integrity to become a cleric. The particular monks Augustine is writing about had left their community without the permission of their abbot.

Augustine's Ministry[1]

Augustine was chosen presbyter of the church of Hippo in 391 and bishop in 395, though he was reluctant to shoulder the burdens, preferring his quiet monastic and philosophical life at Thagaste. He wrote to his bishop Valerius (L 21), concerning his feelings about the clerical calling. First of all, he is shocked that some seek the office of bishop, presbyter or deacon just to obtain the honor and flattery of the people.

---

1. See M. Pellegrino, *The True Priest—The Priesthood as Preached and Practiced by Saint Augustine*, tr. A. Gibson (Villanova: Augustinian Press, 1988). Pellegrino was a great help in researching this chapter.

There is nothing in this life more difficult, more laborious or more dangerous that the office of bishop, presbyter or deacon. But nothing more blessed in the sight of God, if he carries on the campaign in the way described by our Commander.

Augustine was urged on by the people of Hippo to become their helmsman before he had even learned how to row. So he often rushed into reprimands without first acknowledging his own mistakes and those of his fellow clergy. But now that he knows his own faults, he seeks remedies in scriptures, prayer and reading so that the grace of the priesthood may be granted to him. Yet he still feels weighed down.

If I have learned by experience what is needful for a man who administers the sacrament and the word of God to the people—do you, Father Valerius, give me a command to my destruction?

Though Valerius thinks Augustine worthy to be a presbyter, his protégé knows better. For even if he possesses a strong faith, necessary for his own salvation, "How am I to make use of this for the salvation of others?" (1 Cor 10:33). It is difficult to live with a safe conscience in the midst of sinners. No one can do this without the help of the Lord through prayer, reading and weeping.

Though Augustine looked forward to spending more time in philosophizing and writing, as he did at Cassiciacum and Thagaste, "once the burden of ecclesiastical authority was laid on me, all those sweet delights slipped away from my hands." So he cannot even find the manuscript he had been working on at the request of a friend (L 101).

The Lord told Peter and his successors to feed his flock. So Augustine's flock should listen to him with obedience, "seeing that we on our part with fear hear 'feed my sheep.' If we feed with fear and fear for the sheep, how ought these sheep to fear for themselves" (S 46). While carefulness and watchfulness are Augustine's portion, obedience and humility are theirs.

Although Augustine speaks from a high place, with fear he is really beneath their feet. For he knows what a grievous account he must render to God.

In Augustine's flock are those learned in the liberal arts and literature, and those nourished by the word of God (S 133). "If I labor in explaining what I mean, do you aid me both by the attention of your hearing and the thoughtfulness of your meditation." But he cannot help them unless he, in turn, is helped. So Augustine encourages a certain synergism of pastor and flock. "Pray we mutually for one another, and look equally for our common Succour."

Augustine writes humbly to his spiritual father and adviser Jerome (L 82). Though as a bishop Augustine ranks higher than his presbyter friend, "in many things I rank lower than Jerome." Furthermore, one should never reject correction on the part of an inferior. Augustine adds that he is afraid to read Jerome's new Latin translation of the scriptures in the liturgy lest he shock his conservative listeners who are used to the old Latin version.

Augustine had always suffered from ill health. While recuperating in 410, he wrote back to his flock in Hippo (L 122). He is sorry that he cannot serve them as he should, "which my fear and love of him press me to render to you." He encourages them to keep up their faith and works of charity and not to become too worldly or too frightened of impending disasters. For though Augustine is away, God is always present to them.

Augustine was kept busy ministering the word and mystery, including the eucharist, baptism, penance, blessing marriages, instructing the catechumens and competentes during Lent, the Easter Vigil and the Easter Octave. Sunday he celebrated the eucharist and gave a homily. And besides his regular preaching on Sundays and feasts and his commentaries on scriptures, he wrote many works challenging heretics.

Augustine frequently was called to service outside of his own diocese, for example, to councils at Carthage and to the election and consecration of African bishops. Moreover, he even had to judge secular cases at his tribunal (*episcopalis audientia*).[1] We discussed in an earlier essay the common life he lived with his clerics at Hippo.[2]

Augustine always kept his head on straight, not lording it over his people. "For God has placed me here as a minister, not as an overseer." And although he may chide, rebuke, anathematize and excommunicate, he does not correct them (S 224). For neither planting nor watering amount to much without God who gives the increase (see 1 Cor 3:7).

But he still finds the bishopric a heavy burden (S 339). So that he worries over it day and night. Though it merits a great reward, if done faithfully, infidelity earns severe punishments. This is more important than the ephemeral applause of his congregation or how they live. He does not want the flattery of the bad livers and he should be indifferent to the praises of the good.

"Lift up my burden and help me to carry it." As Christmas nears with the customary feeding of the poor, Augustine notes that his words are spiritual food. For it is not enough just to hand out visible victuals. So he feeds his people a supernatural diet, and, at the same time, is fed from the storehouse of God. "I am your minister, not your *pater familias.*" He serves them from the Lord's treasury, from the feast of his *pater familias*, Jesus Christ.

As we have seen, Augustine longs for his former leisurely life of philoso-

---

1. The *episcopalis audientia* was recognized by the state. Though originally it was concerned with spiritual and clerical matters, eventually the bishops also arbitrated lay disputes in cooperation with the state courts. The authority of the episcopal courts varied with the times until settled by Justinian (C 1, 4; Nov 123). See Berger, *Encyclopedic Dictionary*, 454.
2. See J. Mohler, *Late Have I Loved You* (New York: New City Press, 1991), chap. 6.

phizing and writing. For nothing is better or sweeter than to study the divine treasures without disturbance. "To preach, argue, correct, build, to be troubled for each one of you is a big job, a big burden and a big work. Who would not flee this responsibility?"

But Augustine does not want to be like the unfaithful servant in the gospel story (see Lk 19:21-23). So he continues to exhort his flock to change for the better. For when someone who was bad yesterday becomes good today, "this is my pay."

On the anniversary of his consecration Augustine again speaks of his burden and how he needs Christ's and his people's help in order to carry it. So he asks them to pray for him and also for themselves. "Support me according to the apostle's recommendation that we bear each other's burdens and so fulfill the law of Christ" (see Gal 6:2) (S 340).

Though he trembles at his heavy responsibility for them, he is consoled that they are with him. "For you I am a bishop, with you I am a Christian." In the first is found duty and danger, while in the second is grace and salvation.

Augustine delights that he is redeemed along with his flock by Christ. But he is also called to be their *praepositus.* At the Lord's command, he will be their servant and a coservant of Christ. Moreover, like Peter, it is Augustine's love of Christ that motivates his care and feeding of his sheep.

Furthermore, it is not due to Augustine's many talents that he feeds his flock, but rather it is owed to the grace of God (see 1 Cor 15:10). "Nevertheless, because we love gratis, because we feed the sheep, we seek a reward." But how can this be? "A reward is not asked by him who freely loves, unless it is he who is loved." How much we owe God for our own pastorate! While our evil is our own doing, our goodness comes from God, for without his grace we cannot act morally. This also holds true for Augustine's church. Though we may plant and water externally, God within grants us our increase in virtue.

While the disturbers need correcting; the weak, consolation; the sick, support; the negative, affirmation; the insidious, warning; the ignorant, education; the lazy, stimulation; "in all these things help us, praying and obeying, so that we desire not so much to preside over you as to be helpful to you" *(non tam praeesse quam prodesse).*

While a bishop should pray for his people, they, in turn, should pray for him (see Col 4:3). Augustine asks for their obedience and salvation. "We pray that our episcopate may be profitable for us and you. So I may tell you what to do, and you may do it. Thus we may come with the help of the Lord to eternal life."

Augustine continues to worry over his flock (L 124), whom he was sent to serve. They are so weak that the slightest breeze bowls them over. "Who is weak and I am not weak?" (2 Cor 11:29). Some even plotted against

Augustine in his absence, "raging against us, while we are busy trying to save them." They are heading for spiritual death, unless he can forestall it.

It was not for love of money that Augustine assumed the heavy obligations of his bishopric.

> God is my witness that it is only because of the service which I owe to the love of my brethren and the fear of God that I bear with that administration of church affairs over which I am supposed to love to exercise authority. But I am so far from loving it that I long to be free of it, if I could do so without failing my duty.

Augustine describes his church as a trinity including: himself, his flock and Christ (S 101). "My place accordingly it is—with all my unworthiness, the Lord has appointed me to be a laborer in his field, and to say these things to you," to sow, plant, water, dig and fertilize.

While it is Augustine's job to be faithful in these duties, it is their obligation to faithfully receive them. Pray to the Lord "to aid me in my labor, and you in your belief, all of us laboring, but in him overcoming the world." No doubt his audience has little interest in Augustine's personal problems. Certainly he has already told them about their own. So why go on and on?

"I think it is better that in a reciprocal and mutual love we should belong to you. You are now, indeed, one family. We of the same family are dispensers, it is true. But we all belong to one Lord." Though Augustine is a dispenser, he does not give from his own wellspring, "but of his from whom I also receive." Moreover, if he claims that his word comes from himself, he is a liar.

Furthermore, his people should be willing to listen to his problems, for some of them might become future dispensers. Whereas Augustine is now giving out spiritual food from a higher station to his congregation, just a few years ago he was "in a lower place, receiving food along with my fellow servants."

The Lord gave his apostles instructions for their ministry. Do not bring along your purse, bag, sandals, etc. (see Lk 10:4-6). These all have spiritual meanings. Thus the purse enclosing money is concealed wisdom. So the bishop should share his wisdom with his flock. Sandals made out of animal skins are dead works. We cannot walk barefoot without helping each other through mutual charity. Saluting means preaching the gospel for Christ and not out of self-interest. The genuine preacher will be received into the homes of the faithful.

Fellow Servant of Christ

Augustine frequently calls himself a fellow servant or fellow disciple of Christ, along with his flock and not above or ahead of them. He is far from the later bishops who wielded temporal power and possessed much wealth, though he sometimes had to make judgments in civil matters besides his many other duties (*episcopalis audentia*).

Thus he writes to the monks that these obligations prevent him from doing physical work or spending as much time in prayer as he would have liked (*The Work of the Monks*, chap. 29). Though distasteful, Augustine assumes judgment even in worldly matters.

> For we are servants of his Church and especially of the weaker members. No matter how weak is our contribution to the mystical body, I pass over the other numberless ecclesiastical cares which only he who is experienced can appreciate.

Augustine does not want to be like a Pharisee who lays heavy obligations on others, but not on himself. Though we all have burdens of our own rank and office, yet our tasks are made lighter by Christ who went through the same travail.

> If you are our brothers, our sons, if we are your fellow servants, or, rather, servants of Christ, hear our advice, understand our precepts, take our suggestions.

However, if Augustine commands them like an insincere Pharisee, they should still do what he says, "even though you do not approve of our actions" (see Mt 23:3). He speaks to them out of his brotherly love. "Let him judge who granted us the opportunity to offer what is worthy in his eyes."

Popular opinion honors those who devote their lives to others, rather than to themselves. For example, "popularity is not obtained by those who are highest in the Church, unless they expose themselves to the toils and hazards of the active life" (*Against Faustus* 22, 56). Quiet pursuit of wisdom and meditation earn no plaudits except when they are pointed toward useful business. For example, the diligent student gains no attention unless he uses his powers for ecclesiastical administration. When studious men "minister in sincerity the mystery of God" so as to beget sons in the faith, popular approval is also gained for their previous years of study.

Augustine and his church cooperate on their way to salvation—co-stewards, co-sheep, co-disciples of Christ, the Good Shepherd (*On the Psalms* 126, 2). Augustine is not the supreme ruler of the vineyard, hiring and firing at will, but rather a co-worker (S 49). "I work in the vineyard according to the strength the Lord has deigned to give me." When he works within his soul, the Lord alone sees. Paul remarked (1 Cor 4:3), "With me it is a small thing that I should be judged by you," for it is the Lord alone who can judge.

> Though you hear my words, you cannot see into my heart. We offer our heart to God to see and we work from our spirit. We do not offend our Teacher, so that with a free countenance we may receive our reward.

We Talk; God Teaches[1]

In his sermons on scriptures Augustine reminds his hearers that he is only an instrument of God's word. The authority of scriptures "was dispensed to us through mortal men whose fame is still spreading abroad, now that they are dead" (*On the Psalms* 103, 1-4). The Holy Spirit, who inspires, walks above the wings of the winds, and above love itself.

"Who makes spirits his angels and flaming fire his ministers," that is, those who are spiritual. "He makes his angels by sending them to preach the gospel." And unless his minister is a fiery preacher, how can he enflame his listeners?

Augustine teaches a necessary symbiosis between the preacher and his audience (*On the Psalms* 103, 46). Thus while the Lord gives Augustine understanding and the power of language, to his flock he offers attention and hearing. "In your conversations stir up this heavenly food." Keep the treasure on your lips.

> For these matters have been sought out and discovered with great labor. With great labor have they been announced and discoursed on.
> May our toil be fruitful to you, and may our soul bless the Lord.

Augustine imitates Paul, insisting that what they hear is not his words, but God's (see 2 Cor 4:7) (S 51). "May he, beloved, fulfill your expectations, who has awakened them."

Earlier Augustine had spoken to a hostile audience who had come merely for the celebration of the feast. But today his hearers are more receptive since their lukewarm brethren are away entertaining themselves at the shows. "We are ministers of the word, not our own word, but the word of our God and Lord, whom no one serves without glory, whom no one despises without punishment" (S 114).

God spoke through the patriarchs, through Christ, through the scriptures, lector and commentator. "If Christ is silent, I could not speak to you" (S 17).

"Nor is Christ silent in your voices. For when you sing, he speaks. He is not silent. So we must listen with the ears of our hearts. It is easy to hear with our bodily ears. However, we attend with our ears of hearing (see Mt 13:9), that is, the ears of obedience."

The presbyters who vigilantly and diligently minister the words of God should be heard (S 20). For our Lord speaks through their truth. Although the bishop is the main preacher, he can delegate this ministry to his presbyters. For example, Bishop Valerius of Hippo invited his presbyter Augustine to preach because of Augustine's ability and his own weakness.

Augustine calls his explication of scriptures a feeding of his flock which should share this delicious bread with others by their good works (S 95).

---

1. This and the following section appeared first in *Pastoral Life*, February/March, 1991.

"What I deal out to you is not my own. What you eat, I eat; what you live upon, I live upon. We have in heaven a common storehouse, whence comes the word of God."

His audience should have a tranquil heart, good faith and earnest attention (S 126). "Attend not to me, the poor vessel, but to him who puts the bread in the vessel." With open and faithful minds, they should be able to understand Augustine's words. However, if they cannot comprehend, then they should be patient. God, through his holy gospel proposes the subject matter for Augustine's homily.

Augustine has to admonish his church because that is what God wants him to do (S 125). "God bids, and I admonish because I am admonished. He alarms me, who does not allow me to keep silent. For he exacts from me what he has given." Furthermore, if Augustine keeps quiet about things which should be mentioned, he is an unfaithful servant.

They have heard the word of God. "For you are here gathered together, and are hanging on the word of God's minister." Do not pay attention to Augustine's mouth by which he speaks. "For hungry men do not regard the meanness of the dish, but the preciousness of the food." Though they hear the word of God, temptations will test their hearing. And the Lord will judge them accordingly.

While Augustine may question their words and actions, God examines their inmost thoughts. "Though he has wished me to be a dispenser, the requiring he reserved to himself." Whereas Augustine's job is to admonish, teach and rebuke—to save or condemn is God's.

Augustine asks his people to hear with hunger the Lord's word. "And when I shall have spoken it, you will doubtless with sound taste approve what is placed before you out of the Lord's store" (S 145). The Lord made our rational minds to be satisfied only with himself, yet without full comprehension here below. So he is manifested to us and at the same time hidden. For even the apostle Paul admitted doing things that he should not do (see Rom 7:19), for the flesh and the spirit are in tension.

> You see with what peril this is heard, if it be not understood. You see how it concerns the pastor's office to open the closed fountains and to minister to the thirsty sheep the pure and harmless water. (S 128)

"The fountains of water springing up from eternal life" (see Jn 4:14) are the preachers of the word of God (*On the Psalms* 17, 16).

Some see the good and true prophets, the predecessors of the preachers, as God's clouds, raining snakes on the sinners and fertility on the godly (*On the Psalms* 10, 10). "Not only the prophets, but all who irrigate souls with the word of God may be called clouds."

God opened up the doors of heaven, raining down manna to eat (*On the Psalms* 77, 15). And, indeed, he gives them the bread of heaven which the manna signified. "The bread by means of the evangelical clouds is being rained over the whole earth." The hearts of the preachers are open like the heavenly doors so that the bread of heaven may be preached to a believing and hoping Church.

The clouds of the preachers cannot be compared to the Lord (*On the Psalms* 88, 7-10). Clouds, like the heavens, "are the preachers of the truth: prophets, apostles, announcers of the word of God." Why are preachers called heaven and clouds? Heaven because of the brightness of the truth, and clouds because of the hidden things of the flesh. Clouds are ephemeral. For though we hear a man's voice, we cannot see into his heart.

> The clouds, therefore, are the preachers of the truth in the flesh. . . . We are called clouds on account of the flesh and we are preachers of the truth on account of the showers of the clouds.

Moreover, our cloudy flesh is nothing like the Lord's virgin body. For although Jeremiah, Elijah and John are called sons of God, and "in their character as preachers of God are called clouds," they still cannot be compared with the Son of God.

The Lord preached, sending the "preachers of his own name throughout all the nations of the world." So the word of God was spoken not only in Palestine, but to the Gentiles as well. "On that spot you thundered out of your own cloud, but to scatter rain upon the Gentiles. . . . You sent other clouds." Though the Lord's rain cloud preachers confront waves of opposition, they should not fear, for the Lord rules the seas and calms the waves.

The Lord rains by his own mouth in the gospels. And he rains through his clouds by sending his apostles to preach the truth. The earth, in her turn, has abundantly given of her fruit, so that her harvest now fills the whole world (*On the Psalms* 66, 8).

"The clouds have uttered a voice" (*On the Psalms* 76, 18). These clouds are "the preachers of the word of truth." But God withheld his rain clouds from the bad vineyard (see Is 5:6). However, when the apostles went over to preach to the Gentiles, the clouds spoke. Moreover, the voices from the clouds are like arrows penetrating their ears and piercing their hearts. Furthermore, the clouds, like wheels, have gone about the round world, shaking it up with thunder and lightning, commandments and miracles. The clouds come from the ends of the earth (*On the Psalms* 134, 8), bringing lightning and rain, fear and rejoicing.

Augustine also compares God's preachers to mountains which are similar to the clouds which surround their peaks (*On the Psalms* 35, 8). "The great preachers are the mountains of God." The rising sun, God, first lights up the mountain tops and then gradually the rest of the world. But "think not that the mountains themselves will help you, for they receive what they give, and so give not of their own." So their hope should not rest on the mountain, but on him who lights up the mountain.

Your help comes through the mountains because the scriptures are administered to you through the mountains, through the great preachers of the Truth. However, do not put all your hopes on the mountains.

Through the mountains (the preachers) comes our help, but not from the mountains. Rather it comes from the Lord who made heaven and earth (*On the Psalms* 103, 14).

Great preachers are also like physicians, imitating the Supreme Doctor in healing the sick (*On the Psalms* 87, 9). "Even though they do not cure by their own power, yet by their faithful ministry they assist toward salvation," aiding the living, but not raising the dead. For the grace of God, which enables them to "hear the lessons of salvation from any of its ministers whatever, is most hidden and mysterious."

"Whatever exertions the best preacher of the word and persuader of the truth may make through miracles are like those of the Great Physician." Yet if their listeners are dead, can the physicians raise them up?

While Augustine listens to Bishop Severus preaching, he, in turn, hears Augustine (*On the Psalms* 131, 1). "In charity itself we are all listening to him, who is our one Master in heaven." Augustine's people should try to recall his past sermons, so that he does not have to repeat himself.

When Augustine speaks aloud, Christ teaches silently inside (S 102). "I speak by the sound of my words, while he speaks within by the fear of the thoughts." Christ lives in their hearts, "and it is in his place to teach what I desire to give utterance to."

Members of God's kingdom truly learn from God and not from men (*On John* 26, 7). Though they learn something from men, what they understand is within. "I am pouring a clutter of words on your ears. What is it that I say or that I speak, unless he who is interior reveals it?" While Augustine plants and waters the tree from without, the Creator of the tree is inside, inspiring its growth (see 1 Cor 3:7).

Augustine recommends a tranquil heart, a godly and devout faith and earnest attention. "Attend not to me, the poor vessel, but to him who puts the bread in the vessel. Attend then for a while to what I have said to exhort you to faith, that your mind, imbued by faith, may be capable of understanding." What Augustine speaks may be pleasing, cheering and understandable. And if they do understand they should be happy. If not, they should be patient.

Jesus was told by his Father what he should speak (see Jn 12:49-50). "O that he would grant me to say what I wish," says Augustine, "for my poverty and his abundance straighten me." Although we are sons of God by grace, he is so by nature (S 140).

Augustine asks the prayers of his congregation that their open hearts may be filled (S 52). "For you see what I have undertaken, and not only what, but who I am that have undertaken it, and of what I wish to speak, and where and what my position is." In his corruptible body he wants to gather up his mind from the multitude of things to the one God, Trinity. "That I may see something which I may say about it," so that he may speak words worthy of this most august subject (*On the Psalms* 86, 4). "May he assist me, may he lift it up with me. For I am too infirm in respect to him, and he in respect to me is too mighty."

Augustine discusses classical eloquence and its place in sermons in his *Christian Doctrine* (book 4). Having been a professional teacher of rhetoric, he echoes many of the techniques of Cicero, Quintilian and other Roman rhetors. He also admires Christian homelists including Jesus, Paul, Cyprian and Ambrose.

The preacher should use the subdued style when teaching, the moderate method when condemning or praising. But if we want to persuade recalcitrant wills, then the grand style is most appropriate. Is style more important than proofs of doctrines? "Is the listener to be persuaded to do something, instead of being instructed that he may learn?" Eloquence is natural when we praise God as much as we can. However, if people are replacing the Creator with his creatures, then the grand style is called for.

Augustine does not hesitate to correct his flock, when they need it (*On the Psalms* 63, 17). "Psalm is chanted, gospel read, reader cries, preacher shouts 'We sin, yet God spares.' " "It is better that God teaches us to fear, than man teaches us not to fear." In the name of Christ, both speaker and listener are living. So why not correct now?

Augustine is not afraid to admonish, because God, in turn, admonishes him (S 75). For God does not allow him to remain silent. And even if he forgets to correct his brethren, the temptations and tribulations which he suffers serve as an admonition. They have heard the word of God and are blessed by the Lord. "For you are here gathered together, and are hanging on the word of God's minister." They should not pay too much attention to Augustine's ailing body from which his words come. For hungry persons are more interested in the food than in the container.

God tests us. We gather to praise the word of God. But the temptations of our daily life measure how well we hear it. While Augustine questions their words and actions, God probes their very thoughts. "He knows how you hear and he knows how to require—he who orders me to give." While Augustine is the dispenser, God is the requirer. "To admonish, to teach, to rebuke is ours; but to save and to crown or to condemn and to cast into hell, is not ours."

Good and Bad Pastors

From its beginning the Church has included sinful laity and erring priests and bishops.[1] Why does Christ allow his stainless Bride to include sinners?

---

1. See chapter 4 on the "Marks of the Church."

This is a great mystery yesterday and today. And, as usual, Augustine faces up to the problem. Since, he knows his own weakness, he is tolerant of the mistakes of others, at the same time, not neglecting to correct according to his episcopal duty. Augustine's is one of the few true autobiographies of the saints that we have. Most lives of the saints have been so sanitized and mythologized as to almost deny the basic sinfulness which God, for his own good reasons, has allowed in his Church.

Peter, the Rock, typifies the strength and weakness of Christ's Church (S 26). Moreover, the other apostles, too, showed character flaws at times.

But did not Paul insist on a saintly clergy (*On John* 41, 10)? Paul did not require sinlessness as a prerequisite, for "then everyone would be rejected as unfit and none would be ordained." Rather he said that the candidates for the superintendency be without crime: murder, adultery, fornication, theft, sacrilege, etc. For once one is cleansed of these, he begins to be free. Yet, like Paul, we all have a certain tension between the flesh and the spirit, part free/part slave.

There are many tracts in the Bible that illustrate good and bad shepherds in the Church, as Christ predicted (*On John* 46). Jesus called himself the Good Shepherd. "He would not add 'good' were there not bad shepherds": thieves, robbers and hirelings. The good are signified by the door, doorkeeper, shepherd and sheep, while the bad are: thieves, robbers, hirelings and wolves.

Whereas the good shepherd guards his flock, the hireling flees, though he still can be useful. Who is this hireling who is sinful, yet needed? Paul says that there are some in the office of the Church, "who seek their own and not the things that are Jesus Christ's." For example, those who are after financial gain and honor are hirelings.

Paul singled out his son Timothy as one who served the Church out of love of Christ (see Phil 2:19-21). Augustine notes that there are hirelings in his day, too. "The Lord's fold must have as overseers, both those who are children and those who are hirelings. . . . The overseers who are sons are the shepherds," all members of the one Shepherd, to whom the sheep belong.

However, even the hirelings are helpful to the Church. For although they rule the Church for personal gain, they preach Christ and Christ's voice is heard through them. "The sheep follow not the hireling, but the shepherd's voice, speaking through the hireling." Jesus Christ said of the Pharisees: "Do what they say, not what they do" (Mt 7:16). However, if they teach their own ideas, do not listen.

The hireling does not by his evil conduct "preach from the seat of Christ. He does injury by the evil he does, not by the good that he says." But when we pick the grapes of God's word, we should look out for the thorns of immorality. Through the hireling we can hear the voice of the Good Shepherd. However, we should not imitate the hireling since we are members of the Shepherd. While children await the eternal heritage of their father, the hireling wants his wages now!

It is according to Church order that no one who had to do public penance for a serious crime should be admitted to ordination, or return to or continue in the clergy (Nicaea, can. 10; *Against the Donatists* 10, 45-46). This was commanded to prevent people from doing penance for the purpose of getting an ecclesiastical post.

On the other hand, though David did penance for his serious sin, he remained king. And Peter, who repented his denial of Christ, did not lose his position as leader of the apostles. However, now there is not a question of individual scandal, but whole nations are being lost. Augustine asks heretical clergy to repent like Peter and so become shepherds in the Catholic Church, which welcomes them. Let peace and charity prevail.

Some degraded clergy have joined certain heresies such as the Donatists (*Against the Letters of Petilian* 3, 37-38). Good and bad shepherds are mixed in the Catholic Church. However, if you are baptized by a bad pastor, just do not imitate him. Your baptism is valid since whether the minister is good or bad, it is Christ who really baptizes and justifies.

Augustine writes to Felicia, a Christian virgin shocked by the life-style of her prelate (L 208). He begins with Paul, "Who is weak and I am not weak? Who is scandalized and I am not on fire?" (2 Cor 11:29).

Christ predicted that scandals would come into his Church. "However, woe to him by whom the scandal comes" (Mt 18:7). Who are these scandalizers? Those who seek their own selfish gain rather than Christ's (see Phil 7:21).

If bad clergy were tolerated by Paul, how much more so should we bear them today? For Christ alone can separate the good from the bad. He instructed us never to abandon the unity of the Church, "because we are offended by the scandals of the chaff." Let our charity carry us through to the final harvest.

We should not even place our hopes in the good shepherds, but rather in the Father. Though Jesus Christ saw many of the scribes and Pharisees as bad shepherds, he also said that their teachings were good, but their actions should not be copied (see Mt 23:2-3). "Even under bad shepherds the sheep are nourished in the Lord's pasture."

However, if you follow a good shepherd, you can imitate both his words and his actions. Yet it is the sinless Christ who is our Good Shepherd, to whom we should attach ourselves (see 1 Cor 1:12-13). "Never forsake the pastures of unity because of the sons of iniquity." Keep hope in the Lord and "you will not be troubled by the scandals which will abound until the end." You will be saved by your devotion to the Lord and his unity.

Peter's threefold denial was healed by his triple confession of love, for which Christ gave him his pastorate. "Let it be the office of love to feed the Lord's flock, as it was the signal of fear to deny the Shepherd" (*On John* 123, 5).

Some seek their own profit, rather than Christ's in the clerichood, "from the desire either of boasting, wielding power, or acquiring gain, and not from the love of obeying, serving and pleasing God." If you love me, you will feed my sheep, not yourself. My love over self-love.

Paul (see 2 Tim 3:1-5) describes the self-lovers: money-grubbing, wicked, blasphemers, etc. This self-interest is especially to be avoided by those who feed Christ's sheep.

Christ died for his sheep, as did many of his martyrs. How much more so should those "who are entrusted by him with the feeding, that is, the teaching and governing of these very sheep," imitate the Good Shepherd. In the one flock, "the shepherds themselves are likewise sheep." For the Good Shepherd, himself, even became a sheep for us, the Lamb of God.

Paul speaks of men in the Church who preach the gospel on occasion, seeking from men their own advantage, whether of money, honor or human praise (see Phil 1:18, 2:21). They have little interest in the salvation of their congregation, but rather in their own advantage. However, the people should still listen to their words, while ignoring their actions (S 137).

The attitude of the good Christian lay person should be, "Let me walk in the way of the Lord and not follow this man's conversation. Let me hear from him, not his words, but God's. I will follow God; let him follow his lust."

People tend to use their erring clerks as excuses for their own misconduct. If he can do it, why can't I? Christ will remind them of what he said about the scribes and Pharisees (see Mt 23:2-3). When a sinner hears a rebuke from the pulpit, he is liable to reply, "The very bishops and clergy do not do it, and you expect me to do it?"

Some bishops even turn around the Lord's words to ensure that the laity obey their bad clergy. "For we can offer sacrifice and you cannot." The Pharisees laid heavy burdens on the people, but not on themselves. Jesus was speaking not only of the scribes and Pharisees, but also of later shepherds, as well.

Those who preach chastely, preach for the love of God. However, "whether by occasion, or in truth, Christ is preached" (Phil 1:18). Christ allows hirelings, who preach for their own personal profit in his Church. Even Paul could find few shepherds such as Timothy among the hirelings of his day.

Presbyters and bishops from their high places teach us sin. Can a Pharisee say good things? Can we gather grapes from thorns? The vine of truth grows on the thorn bush of the Pharisees. But do what they say (grapes) and not what they do (thorns).

Some even petition false judgments from a bishop in order to settle a legal matter. And so they flatter him. However, Augustine responds, "I seek nothing from you, but your salvation." Thus he groans over their sins and reproves their faults.

Furthermore, he repents over his own mistakes, for priests are not sinless. "First offer sacrifice for your own sins and so for the people" (Lv 16; Hb

7:27). In the Old Law the priests' sacrifices witnessed to their sins. For they would not offer oblations if they had not erred (S 135).

Augustine adds: "God willed me to be a priest, yet I am a sinner." So along with his flock he asks God's pardon and mercy. Even the apostles made mistakes, for they said the Lord's prayer frequently (see Mt 6:9-12). "They come in debtors, go out absolved and return debtors to prayer, since this life is not without sin." But as often as the Lord's prayer is said, sins are forgiven.[1] Did the apostles even sin after they had received the Holy Spirit on Pentecost Sunday? "If we say we have no sin, the truth is not in us" (1 Jn 1:8). But if we confess, God will forgive us.

There is a danger in pride among those who teach (L 266). And how much more so among those who teach divine truth. However, there is much pleasure in seeing our scholars advance. Paul was cured of his temptations toward pride by a thorn pricking his flesh (see 1 Tim 2:7). Also we should remember that the Lord is our only rabbi and master (see Mt 23:8-10). And Paul reminds us that it is God who gives the increase (see 1 Cor 3:7). Christ, our interior master, is our main teacher.

Ezekiel (34:1-16) is a favorite passage of Augustine. For here the prophet criticizes the shepherds of Israel who are more intent on feeding themselves than their sheep. They eat well, but they do not protect the weak or try to find the lost. Without a shepherd, the sheep are scattered and devoured by wild beasts. But the Lord will take away the shepherds' authority and rescue, feed, pasture and heal his sheep (S 46). Even today some want the name and prestige of the clergy, not, however, the responsibilities.

We bishops are Christians for ourselves and leaders for others. Augustine asks the Lord's help in order to speak the truth in his sermons. For if we teach only our own ideas, we are feeding ourselves. However, if we speak God's words, we feed our sheep. Whereas most Christians carry an easier burden along the path to eternal life, bishops shoulder a heavier load. And so Augustine asks his people for their prayers of encouragement.

When a bishop comes to judgment, he is questioned about how he served his flock, whether he worked for his own reward or theirs, whether he fed himself or his Church. While a bad shepherd drinks the fresh milk and wears the fine wool produced by his sheep, he neglects the sick, the depressed, the strayed and the scattered.

Only he who feeds his flock deserves its milk (see 2 Thes 3:8). Yet it is not proper for people to pay those who serve them in the charity of the gospel. For salvation is their reward. Wool is honor, while milk is food. Both are sought from the people by those who feed themselves rather than their sheep.

But all of us are weak, even bishops. For a bishop is only flesh and blood. He eats, sleeps, rises, is born and dies. In a word, a bishop is only a man. So if you honor him as an angel, "you cover up what is weak in him."

---

1. See chapter 7 on the medicinal Lord's Prayer.

Paul and Augustine say: "My food is salvation, my honor is salvation." Even the great Paul was not always well received by his people (see Gal 4:14-16). And although he accepted milk and wool from his flock, he never sought his own interest over Christ's.

Like Paul, the good pastor should not spare the vices of his people just to keep in their good graces. For example, if Augustine preaches the easy way, he will attract huge audiences. If we feel that the people may not understand, we prefer to offend the few, while conciliating the many, speaking our own words rather than those of Christ and God, pastors in our own interest, rather than our sheep's.

The vices of his sheep are patent to their pastor. For the fat and healthy sheep are few and well nourished with the food of truth. Bad pastors care little for the weak, infirm, erring and lost. Furthermore, they try to slay even the strong and stout sheep. How do they kill them? By their bad example.

Even the good sheep ask, "If my boss acts thus, who am I not to do what he does?" Thus the bad pastor kills the strong, and a fortiori, the weak. However, though the pastor may be dead, the sheep are safe because the Lord still lives. Besides the dead pastors who seek their own gain, there are many good pastors who, wanting only Christ's interest, feed their sheep rather than themselves.

But why does not the Lord take his sheep away from the bad pastors and give them to the good shepherds? It is a mystery why God allows good and bad ministers in his Church. But the fact that he does permit this is clear. So when you refuse to do what the bad pastor says, he does not feed you. And when you do do it, Christ feeds you. Hear the preacher who says: do not steal. But do not imitate his theft.

We find that all good pastors are in one Pastor. Out of many apostles, Christ chose one to feed his sheep. Moreover, if there are good sheep, there are also good shepherds. Why? "Because from the good sheep come the good shepherds," who are in the one good Pastor. They feed and, at the same time, Christ feeds. These friends of the Bridegroom do not speak with their own voice, but they rejoice in the voice of the Bridegroom. These good pastors glory in Christ. For Christ, in Christ and with Christ, they feed their sheep.

It is against the Donatists that Augustine perfects his theology of sin and sinners in the clergy (*Against the Letters of Petilian* 2, 30). For one to be a true priest he should receive the sacrament of ordination and also be right-eous. However, if one is a priest in virtue of the sacrament alone, he is like the high priest Caiaphas, who persecuted the one, true Priest. "Yet what he gives is true, if he gives not what is his own, but what is God's."

Paul quotes a foreign prophet because what he said is true (see Tit 1:12-13). So we should distinguish between the faults in us and the truth of God. Paul even found an altar to the unknown God among the pagan shrines in Athens. But because Paul discovered truth among the sacrilegious, does not mean that he approved of their wickedness. "So it is wrong to despise the sacraments of God because of the faults of men." Thus we accept the sacraments of the Donatists without approving their schism.

What about the good tree which produces luscious fruit, while the bad tree gives a spoiled and wormy crop (see Mt 7:16-17; Mt 12:35)? Does this imply that someone who is baptized by an immoral priest becomes bad? Actually, the tree signifies the human being, while the fruit is ones ethical conduct. So the newly baptized are not the fruit of the officiating cleric, but of Christ. For example, Apollos and Paul are only ministers of Christ (see 1 Cor 3:4-5). So also Donatus, Januarius and Petilianus are servants of God who gives the increase.

"For ministering and dispensing the word and sacrament, Paul is something, but for purifying and justifying he is nothing," since Christ does this (3, 54).

A minister, therefore, that is a dispenser of the word and sacrament of the gospel, if he is a good man, becomes a fellow partner in the working of the gospel. But if he is bad, he does not, therefore, cease to be a dispenser of the gospel. If he is good, he gives the word and sacrament of his own free will. However, if he is bad, be offers the word and sacrament unwillingly and only for his own personal gain (see 1 Cor 9:17). And if I am good and announce the good, I receive good for myself. On the other hand, even if I am bad, "I still announce what is good." And so I am yet a dispenser of the gospel. Though Judas was bad, he announced the good news; and those who heard him were justified by Christ.

Like the rabbis, Paul begets disciples. However, he raises them up not through his own teachings, but rather through the gospels (see 1 Cor 4:15). Moreover, even if he had preached out of selfish motives, his disciples would have received the gospel message. Furthermore, if we can receive the gospel from an evil minister, how much more also baptism.

We have seen in this chapter the ministers of Christ's Church, channels of his word and sacrament, who should be humble, rather than lording it over their flocks. Augustine begs for the prayers of his Church to help him bear the burdens of his office. Furthermore, he asks them not to pay attention to himself and his fancy words, but rather to the teachings of Christ which he preaches. He also treats of the perennial problem of sinful clergy. Echoing Jesus, Augustine replies: do what they say, not what they do. In the following chapter we will discuss several important sacraments of the Church, namely, baptism, the eucharist and penance.

VII.

YOU ARE WHAT YOU HAVE RECEIVED

(Sermon 227)

The Sacraments

Christ himself, God incarnate, is the sacrament par excellence, whose fullness is found in the Church, which ministers individual sacraments to the faithful. What is a sacrament? "A visible sacrifice is a sacrament or sacred sign of an invisible sacrifice," remarks Augustine (*The City of God* 10, 5).

In Augustine's day the word "sacrament" was used of many rituals including instructions in the creed, the Lord's Prayer, exorcism, the eucharist, etc. The true minister of the sacraments is Christ who works through his Church. So sinful ministers do not affect the efficacy of the sacrament, as we have seen in the previous chapter.

The Church bears her children in her womb, and in the womb of her handmaids, "by virtue of the same sacraments as though by virtue of the seed of her husband" (*On Baptism Against the Donatists* 1, 10). Besides grace, some sacraments such as baptism and order give an indelible character so that they cannot be repeated.

Grabowski[1] notes that the sacraments are visible signs of the Church. Moreover, they are not only symbols of individual sanctification, but also signify Church unity and spiritual communion. All religions need external signs or rites for the sake of unity. "The importance of these sacraments cannot be overestimated" (*Against Faustus* 19, 11-14).

The sacraments of the Old Testament are types of those to come. For example, the ark and baptism. The Maccabees refused to violate the Hebrew sacramental food laws. "How much more should a Christian in our day be ready to suffer all things for Christ's baptism, for Christ's eucharist, for Christ's sacred sign," since these are what the former sacraments of the Old Law foretold. By faith, signs and sacraments we will have Christ with us now and we will have him always (*On John* 51, 13).

Augustine sums it up (L 54):

Jesus Christ laid on the society of his new people the obligation of

---

1. Grabowski, *The Church*, 176.

sacraments, very few in number, very easy of observance, most sublime in their meaning. For example: baptism, hallowed by the name of the Trinity; communion of his body and blood; and whatever else is commanded in the canonical writings.

Other observances, for example, the celebration of the major feasts of our Lord are passed down to us from the apostles and Church councils. Other customs vary with the locality. For example, some churches celebrate the eucharist daily, while others come together on Saturdays and Sundays, or only on Sundays.

Baptism in the Name of the Trinity

All cultures have initiation rites, usually at the time of puberty and including some sort of purification and ritual death along with instructions in tribal myths. Often baptism is part of the cleansing rite, recapitulating cosmic origins out of the primeval waters. The individual dies to his childhood and is reborn a full fledged tribal member.

Jewish baptism of proselytes along with circumcision, sacrifice and instruction partook of this ancient practice, with Gentiles being reborn as Jews. Also immersion was practiced by the Qumran monks and the Baptists in the Jordan valley.

The Gentile baptism as taught by Jesus Christ (see Mt 28:18-20) is a spiritual rebirth by the Holy Spirit (Acts 10:47). Though Christians abandoned circumcision, instruction in the mysteries remained an essential part of their initiation. And the Fathers taught that baptism is a recapitulation of the life-giving primordial waters of creation.

In his *The Sacraments*, Ambrose, Augustine's mentor, shows the types of baptism in scriptures. For example, the Jordan River, the flood, the Red Sea, the healing pool in Jerusalem, etc. If these types have cleansing power, a fortiori, their antitype (2, 5). We are baptized three times in honor of the Trinity, dying and rising with Christ. "God anointed you, the Lord sealed you and placed the Holy Spirit in your heart" (2 Cor 1:21-22) (6, 2).

Augustine wrote more on baptism than on any other sacrament because of his problems with the Donatists who questioned the baptism administered by unworthy clergy. However, as we have seen, Christ is the invisible minister of the sacraments, while clerics are the visible ones.

The baptized receive a seal not unlike that of a Roman slave or soldier. Thus baptism cannot be repeated. Just as the good shepherd marks his sheep so that they can be identified in case they are lost or stolen, "so the wandering of the sheep is to be remedied without destroying in it the mark of the redeemer" (L 185). Even in desertion Christians keep their royal mark and so can be received back in the Church without rebaptism. Should they be forced to return? Why not? Jesus Christ forced Paul!

What about infant baptism? There was a long tradition in the Church of adult baptism, except when whole families were converted, perhaps reflecting Jewish proselyte baptismal customs. Obviously a child cannot make a decision for conversion, so the family or church has to decide for him or her.

Augustine feels that there are two reasons why infants need baptism. First, they are born in sin and, secondly, they should be cleansed in order to receive their heavenly food (*On the Forgiveness of Sin and Baptism* 1, 25).[1] Of course, a baptized infant can turn out bad later. However, if he or she dies after baptism, eternal life is the reward.

Christ gave his bread for the life of the world (see Jn 6:51), which includes infants, who need baptism to prepare themselves for the life-giving eucharist. Augustine says that the helplessness of babies corresponds to their weak minds in their sinful flesh. Moreover, their concupiscence is not entirely removed by baptism.

Baptism and the eucharist (salvation and life) remove the guilt of sin from infants (see Job 14:4; Ps 51:5) (1, 33). Since Christ died also for the tiny ones. So unless they are baptized, they remain in darkness. Augustine quotes scripture to show that because all are involved in original sin, all need cleansing (1, 39).

Besides its saving and liberating goal, baptism has a social purpose, namely, incorporating one into the body of Christ. But is it possible to become a member of the Church without baptism? For example, Cyprian says that martyrs received the crown, even if unbaptized (*On Baptism* 4, 11).[2] And Cornelius received the Holy Spirit before he was baptized (Acts 10:44).

Can a catechumen be more righteous than a bad baptized person? Besides baptism, we need a spirit of conversion. We should never depreciate the morality practiced before baptism, nor despise the baptism of heretics. However, baptism is of no avail toward salvation, "unless he who has been baptized to full perfection, is incorporated into the Church," and rectifies his own depravity. So such a one should be corrected (4, 21).

Infants also are incorporated into the Church at their baptism. So "they are united with the body and members of Christ" (*On the Forgiveness of Sin and Baptism* 3, 7).

Although one may be good and prayerful like Cornelius, it cannot be to his benefit, "unless he is welcomed into the Church by the bond of Christian brotherhood and peace" (*On Baptism* 1, 8). So Cornelius, after his baptism by Peter "was joined by the tie of communion to the fellowship of Christians, to which he was bound before only by the likeness of good works."

The good thief on the cross was saved without baptism. And so also the martyrs and converts (see Rom 10:10). However, "the want is supplied

---

1. The next few quotes are from here.
2. Unless otherwise noted quotes in this section from here.

invisibly only when the administration of baptism is prevented—by the necessity of the moment." But there is always a danger of pride, namely, feeling that, though unbaptized, one is superior in virtue to the baptized (4, 22).

Can anyone at all be baptized? Augustine addresses this problem in his *Faith and Works* (413). During the fifth century the applicant was generally questioned about his or her motives for requesting baptism. For example, to get out of a bad marriage or to get a better position in the community, to supply the church with produce or manufactured goods, etc.

After some instruction, the inquirer declares his or her sincerity and belief in what had been explained, promising to live according to Christian morals. Then he or she receives the sign of the cross, the laying on of hands and exorcism and becomes a catechumen for two or three years, attending their proper liturgy and reading the scriptures.

When ready for baptism, the catechumen applies at the beginning of Lent as a competent to be instructed by the bishop in the Christian mysteries during the Lenten season, receiving also: scrutiny, exorcism, the laying on of hands and insufflation. A special ceremony imparts the creed of baptism. The competent then learns the creed and the Lord's Prayer.

Easter morning brings baptism, the profession of faith and holy communion. Then during Easter week special instructions are given on these two great sacraments. Finally, on Low Sunday he or she lays aside the white garment, recites the Lord's Prayer with the congregation and becomes a full member of the Church.[1]

Augustine objects to laxity in the preparation of the catechumens. For example, accepting those who are unwilling to reform their lives. So even the adulterous, concubinous and fornicators are admitted to baptism. He feels that some are misinterpreting the scriptural passages that say that the kingdom of God includes sinners. Others say baptize them first and then instruct in faith and morals. Of course, this is legitimate when there is a danger of death. However, they cannot continue in their old ways, once they are reborn as Christians.

Though some say that adulterers, idolaters and murderers should be excommunicated, other churches admit adulterers to baptism, although sometimes unwittingly (19). Due to a sense of overconfidence at times anyone at all is accepted for baptism, since baptism forgives all sin anyway (26). But Augustine believes that sinners should first be instructed in the morals of the Church and continue to live a reformed way afterwards in order to attain eternal life.

Is the external immersion enough if it is properly administered? Though it is valid, it is not necessarily fruitful. So even baptism outside of the Church is valid, though it is not fully effective until one joins the Church of Christ.

1. S. M. Liguori, F 15:216-17.

Are the sins of the baptized forgiven? Yes. Furthermore, "sins which are forgiven afterwards to those who pray and repent, are forgiven them because they have been baptized" (*On the Creed*, chap. 8).

However, those who receive baptism outside of the Church are like deserters from the army who still wear their seal of service, but without grace, and are not incorporated into the mystical body of Christ.[1] So one who is baptized by heretics, receives the form of the sacrament, but not the life of grace inspired by the Holy Spirit. Why is their baptism valid? Because Christ administers the sacrament. And when they enter the body of Christ, they receive the grace of the Holy Spirit.

In order to enter the mystical body of Christ one must be reborn of God and the Church (S 121). God gives us grace and justification, while the Church grants us full membership in Christ's body. The Church is our mother and Christ's since she gives birth to his members in baptism (*On Virginity*, chap. 5).

We die because our members are from the first Adam. We live because we are members of the second Adam by a spiritual incorporation (L 187). We need birth and rebirth, while Jesus Christ needed only his birth for us.

By being baptized he gave a higher commendation to the sacrament of our regeneration through his humility, signifying our old man by his passion and our new one by his resurrection.

The Body and Blood of Christ

Most cultures celebrate ritual meals in which food is offered to the gods or spirits, sacrificed and shared in a holy communion. It can also mark a cosmic event such as the *solstice* or *equinox*, or an ancient hierophany like the Passover or the Sabbath, or a pivotal tribal work such as planting, first fruits or harvest, or a life change, that is, birth, puberty, marriage or death.

Judaism celebrated the Sabbath with the *kiddush* and *berakoth* (eucharist), thanking Yahweh for the bread and wine. This was usually observed as a home ritual, although the rabbinical *haburah* also practiced the rite. The Passover Seder celebrates the exodus from Egypt. And the Qumran monks anticipated the Messianic banquet.

Early Christians commemorated the last Passover meal of Jesus and his *haburah*. The eucharist is the fellowship meal of the messianic community, at which the Messiah is really present.

Not only baptism, but also the eucharist is necessary for the life of the Church. That is why after baptism the body and blood of Christ are also received.

---

1. Grabowski, *The Church*, 418-19.

Ambrose, writing on the sacraments (4, 8), shows that the mysteries of the Church are older and more excellent than their Old Testament types, such as the manna. He sees Melchizedek reborn in Christ. "The sacrament which you have received is not a gift of man, but of God," brought forth by Melchizedek who blessed Abraham. Not only are the sacraments of the Church more ancient, but also more powerful. For example, those who ate manna, died, but those who partake of the bread of heaven live forever.

The Church urges us to eat and drink. "Christ is in the sacrament because the body is Christ's. So the food is not corporeal, but spiritual." "The body of God is a spiritual body, the body of Christ is the body of the Divine Spirit, for the Spirit is Christ" (Lam 4, 20).

Ambrose speaks of the eucharist (4, 3).[1] "When consecration has been added—from bread it becomes the flesh of Christ." All the preceding words of the Mass are said by the priest, for example, praise, prayer and petition. "However, when it comes to performing a venerable sacrament, then the priest uses not his own expressions, but he uses the phrases of Christ. Thus the words of Christ perform the sacrament."

"He spoke and they were made" (Ps 148). Before the consecration there was no body of Christ. But after the consecration we have the body of Christ! "He himself commanded and it was created." So we become a new creation after our own consecration in baptism.

If heaven can operate in an earthly fountain (Ps 36:9; Is 41:18) or in other ways, a fortiori, "does it not operate in heavenly sacraments," turning bread and wine into the body and blood of Christ?

"Take and eat of this, all of you, for this is my body. . . . Take and drink of this, all of you, for this is my blood" (Mt 26:26-28) (4, 5). Christ's words change the bread and wine into his body and blood for eternal life. So at communion time when the priest says, "The body of Christ," we reply, "Amen," or "It is true."

"Let him kiss me . . . " (Sg 1:1). "He sees that you are clean of all sin because transgressions have been wiped away. Thus he judges you worthy of the heavenly sacraments and so he invites you to the heavenly banquet" (5, 2). Then we approach the altar to receive the body of Christ, whose sacraments are better than fine wine, celebrating his marriage with his Church, spirit and flesh, spirit and soul.

The Lord is our Good Shepherd who feeds us (Ps 23). We come to the heavenly sacraments, dressed in white, in the garden of the canticle, inebriated by the Holy Spirit (5, 3).

In the Lord's Prayer we ask for our daily bread of eternal life (5, 4). "Receive daily what is of benefit to you daily. So live that you may deserve to receive it daily." However, although the eucharist is a sacrifice, the death and resurrection of the Lord, the elevation of the Lord, the remission of sins,

---

1. The next few quotes from here.

yet we do not receive it daily. "The fact that we are under sin is a wound, whose medicine is the heavenly and venerable sacrament."

Augustine, Ambrose's protégé, notes that the eucharist, like the Church, has visible and invisible elements. The external species he calls *sacramentum,* while the internal, invisible, spiritual part, the body and blood of Christ, the food of life, produces the *res* or *virtus sacramenti* in the soul, paralleling the invisible, spiritual nature of the Church, the mystical body of Christ.[1] Only living, believing members of the mystical body can receive both the *sacramentum* and the *res.*

Christ promises Christians the liberation from their sins through the eucharist (see Jn 6:50-51). "Because these and these alone have eaten not merely the sacramental symbol, but the reality of the body of Christ by reason of the incorporation in his body." "Because the bread is one, we, though many, are one body" (1 Cor 10:17) (see *The City of God* 21, 25).[2]

So he or she who properly eats the body and blood of Christ, "is incorporated in the unity of his body," as a member of Christ, "of the sacrament of whose body the faithful regularly partake when they communicate at the altar." Heretics and schismatics are not in the bond of peace and unity "of which the sacrament is an outward sign."

No one can eat the body of Christ who is outside of the body of Christ. We cannot say that those who formerly were baptized and received the body of Christ will ultimately be saved though they have left the body of Christ. Moreover, those with corrupt morals cannot reach eternal life. For they cannot eat the body of Christ since they are members of a harlot (see 1 Cor 6:15).

Christ said that whoever eats his flesh and drinks his blood "abides in me and I in him" (Jn 6:57).

> Here he shows what is meant by eating Christ's body and drinking his blood, not merely in the outward sacramental sign, but in the reality and truth of remaining in Christ, so that Christ may remain in him who eats and drinks sacramentally.

Thus one who does not abide in Christ and in whom Christ does not live, may not eat Christ's body or drink his blood. For no one can abide in Christ except a member of Christ (21, 25).

> We, the many, are one body in Christ. This is the sacrifice which the Catholic Church continues to celebrate in the sacrament of the altar, in which it is clear to the Church that she herself is offered in the very oblation she makes to God. (10, 6)

When Jesus Christ said that his disciples were to eat his flesh, some

---

1. Grabowski, *The Church,* 183.
2. Unless otherwise noted, quotes in this section are from *The City of God.*

thought that he was encouraging cannibalism. Christ gave us his flesh that he received from Mary for our salvation. "And no one eats that flesh, unless he has first worshipped" (*On the Psalms* 99, 8). However, we are not to chew his skin and muscles, gnaw his bones, and quaff his dripping gore. "I have recommended to you a certain mystery. Spiritually understood, it will quicken." Although it is visually celebrated, "it must be spiritually understood."

Augustine feels that Psalm 33 refers to the eucharist (*On the Psalms* 33, 11). "Now he will speak of the same sacrament, whereby he was carried in his own hands. 'O taste and see that the Lord is good.' " Understand this and you can believe that his flesh and blood gives us life (see Jn 6:53).

Bread and wine are changed into the body and blood of Christ by a sacramental action, a benediction, sanctification, consecration, confection, expressing the relationship between the real body of Christ and his mystical body.[1]

Augustine's Easter sermon (S 227) (F), teaches his flock, especially the newly baptized, about the eucharist, which they will soon receive. "That bread which you see on the altar, consecrated by the Word of God, is the body of Christ," and the wine, also blessed by God's Word, "is the blood of Christ." Under these accidents the Lord hides his body and blood shed for us.

"If you have received worthily, you are what you have received." One bread, one body, though many members (see 1 Cor 10:17). The one bread signifies the unity of the Church, made from many grains of wheat, which are ground, watered and baked. In like manner, the competentes are humbled through their fast and exorcism, watered by baptism and baked with the fire of the chrism of the Holy Spirit.

"Therefore, the fire, that is the Holy Spirit, comes after the water. Then you become bread, that is, the body of Christ," signifying our unity. At the beginning of the canon of the Mass we lift up our heads to Christ our head and give him thanks. And after the consecration of the holy sacrifice, we say the Lord's Prayer because he wished us to be his sacrifice, "which sacrifice is a sign of what we are." Moreover, the kiss of peace anticipates the unity of the eucharist.

But do not receive unworthily (see 1 Cor 11:27). "For these are great and powerful sacraments." What you see, passes. But what you do not see, remains. The body of Christ, the Church of Christ, the members of Christ are not consumed. For what is signified will last eternally. We receive in unity of heart with hope in heaven. Here we believe, while there we will see. The communion of saints originally meant the communion of holy things. But it also can refer to the oneness of the members of the body of Christ.

The body and blood of Christ are called sacraments because they seem to

---

1. Grabowski, *The Church*, 184.

be two things, that is, bread and wine, and are understood to be others, i.e., the body and blood of Christ. Though the corporeal species is seen, it has a spiritual fruit (S 272).

If we are members of the body of Christ (see 1 Cor 12:27), our mystery lies in the Lord's table, where we receive our mystery. If we are truly members of his body, we can respond "Amen" when the priest offers us the eucharist. One bread from many grains, one wine from many grapes. "Thus the Lord consecrated this mystery of our peace and unity in his table." There cannot be unity without peace.[1] While baptism incorporates us into the body of Christ, the eucharist increases this, intensifying our integration in the Church.

Because he died for us, Christ left us an inheritance in the sacrament of his body and blood. "For we have become his body and through his mercy we are what we receive" (S 229) (F). "Behold what you have received!" Just as bread was made into one mass of dough, "so may you also be one body by loving one another, by one faith, hope and undivided charity." To those who would split up the Church into factions, the bread of unity is a testimony against them.

Likewise wine comes from many grapes that have been pressed. "There you are on the table, and there you are in the chalice, for you are one with us. We receive together and drink together because we live together."

Augustine frequently refers to the eucharist as a sacrifice, which was prefigured by Old Testament types. But it is also a heavenly banquet at the Lord's table. Moreover, the eucharistic sacrifice is not confined to one temple as in the Old Law. The Church is a true temple since there is a true sacrifice in every work which unites us in a holy communion with God. That is, "in every work that is aimed at that final good in which alone we can be truly blessed" (10, 6). A *sacrificium* is "something divine." So, if we are vowed to God, we are sacrifices, offering our bodies in spiritual service (see Rom 21:1), and even more so when we offer our souls.

True sacrifices are "works of mercy done to ourselves or our neighbor and directed to God." "The communion of saints is offered as a universal sacrifice to God through the High Priest," who took the form of a servant: mediator, priest and sacrifice. We are the sacrifice, one body in Christ, "which the Church continues to celebrate in the sacrament of the altar, in which it is clear to the Church that she herself is offered in the very offering she makes to God."

Augustine notes (*The Trinity* 3, 4)[2] that Paul preached Christ in four ways: by signs, sermons, letters and by the sacrament of his body and blood. Augustine describes this sacrament as the fruits of the earth "consecrated by

---

1. We discussed the unity of the Church previously in the section in chapter 4 on the "Marks of the Church."
2. Next few quotes are from here.

a mystical prayer and has been duly taken for our spiritual health in memory of the Lord's passion." The people bring the visible elements of bread and wine to the altar. "Yet it is not sanctified so as to be so great a sacrament, except by the Spirit of God, working invisibly."

God effects all that is done by the outward signs of the minister. "Since at the outset he sets the invisible things of his ministers in motion," God also uses visible creatures to show his presence, though he does not appear in his spiritual mysterious substance.

Infants have no knowledge of the eucharistic presence of Christ. For all they see are the physical elements of bread and wine. But if someone of great authority teaches them whose body and blood it is, they believe (3, 10).

Like the disciples at Emmaus (see Lk 24:16), the faithful recognize Christ in the breaking of the bread, which, receiving the blessing of Christ, becomes his body (S 234) (F).

The eucharist played an important role in the life of Monica, Augustine's mother. And her daily devotion to the body and blood of Christ no doubt influenced her son's dedication to the altar. "For she knew that from it would be dispensed that holy victim," through whose sacrifice Satan and sin are blotted out. "By the bond of faith your handmaid bound her soul to the sacrament of our redemption." And when Monica passed away, the sacrament of our redemption was offered for her soul at her graveside, echoing the Roman custom of the *refrigerium* (*Confessions* 9, 12-13).

In the Old Testament Wisdom sends her handmaids to the little ones, saying, "Come, eat my bread, and drink the wine which I have mingled for you" (Prv 9:1-5). Wisdom, God's Word, built himself a house, his body, in the virgin's womb. And he united to himself as head the Church, his members; "slayed" his martyrs as "victims"; and set his table with bread and wine, like Melchizedek, inviting the weak and providing his own body and blood for food and drink. "This offering up of his body and the administration of it to those who communicate supplant all those ancient sacrifices and oblations" (17, 20).

Portalié[1] notes that in the fourth century the word "sacrament" signified the appearance of the bread. So in this sense the sacrament of the eucharist is a figure of the body of Christ (*On the Psalms* 3). Thus we do not touch or break the body of Christ, "but only the sign of that body which is mysteriously present."

But, Augustine warns (*Christian Doctrine* 3, 9), we should not become slaves of the sign, without knowledge of what it means. However, if we use and revere the divinely established sign, whose efficacy and meaning we know, we do not "worship this visible and transitory sign, but—rather that reality, to which such symbols must be ascribed." Thus we can become free even in the midst of our carnal slavery.

---

1. Portalié, *Guide*, 255.

Our Lord Jesus Christ has given us very few observances, for example, baptism and the celebration of his body and blood. And with proper instruction we do not rest satisfied with the symbols instead of the realities which they represent (3, 16). Quoting John (6, 54), "unless you eat the flesh of the Son of Man, etc.," Augustine explains that this is a figure of speech "directing that we are to participate in the Lord's passion and treasure up in grateful and salutary remembrance the fact that his flesh was crucified and wounded for us."

Since Christ is the true vine (see Jn 15:1), his redeeming and vivifying blood is the wine. Noah drank wine, the image of the Lord's passion (see Gn 9:21-23). And Melchizedek offered bread and wine, prefiguring Christ (see Ps 109).

Also Ambrose, speaking of the rock of sacrifice of Gedeon (see Jdg 6:11-21), calls the rock a symbol of Christ, from whom Christians drink (*On the Holy Spirit* 1, Prol.). And just as the angel inflamed Gedeon's sacrifice, so "the flesh of our Lord, animated by the Spirit of God, consumes all the sins of humanity."

Since Jesus said that the Spirit quickens, we understand his words spiritually. So his disciples are not to eat and drink of the physical body which they see. "I have commended to you a certain mystery. Spiritually understood, it will quicken." Although the eucharist is visibly celebrated, "it must be spiritually understood." Thus we eat and drink the body and blood of Christ spiritually in our hearts in faith and in remembrance of Christ's death. Nevertheless, though the presence of Christ in the eucharist is spiritual, it is real.[1]

Jesus Christ calls himself the living bread from heaven, which was foreshadowed by the manna in the desert. "God's altar signified this bread" (*On John* 26, 12-19). These were sacraments, diverse signs, "but in the thing which was signified they were alike." Though we eat and drink different things from our fathers, the spiritual is the same. "They drank from the spiritual rock that followed them, and that rock was Christ" (1 Cor 10:1-4).

What about the living bread from heaven? "This belongs to the virtue of the sacrament, not to the visible sacrament. Thus we eat within and not without, we eat with our hearts and not with our teeth. The manna was just a shadow of the living bread from heaven, the Truth. Can flesh comprehend flesh that is called bread?"

"Believers know the body of Christ, if they neglect not to be the body of Christ. Let them become the body of Christ, if they wish to live in the Spirit of Christ." For no none lives by the Spirit of Christ unless the body of Christ, because the body lives by the Spirit, which gives it life. So if we want to live by the Spirit of Christ, we should be in the body of Christ.

"The body of Christ cannot live but by the Spirit of Christ." One bread, one body (see 1 Cor 10:17). "A mystery of piety! A sign of unity! A bond of

---

1. Portalié, *Guide*, 256.

charity!" "Let him be embodied, that he may be made to live." Let him cleave to the body as a member, not deformed or rotten, but a sound member. "Let him cleave to the body, live for God and by God." Labor now in order to reign in heaven.

Those who eat of the one bread do not fight each other. "For we, being many, are one bread, one body." By this unifying bread "God makes people of one sort who dwell in a house" (Ps 68:6).

Jesus Christ promised eternal life if we eat his flesh and drink his blood. How this happens we do not know. "He would have this meat and drink to be understood as meaning the fellowship of his own body and members," that is, his Church.

The sacrament of the unity of the body and blood of Christ "is prepared on the Lord's table in some places daily, and in some places less often." To some it gives life, to others destruction.

> But the thing itself, of which it is the sacrament, is for every man to life, for no man to destruction, whosoever shall have been a partaker thereof.

This does not mean that our physical bodies will never die. For Jesus Christ promises resurrection and eternal life. This meat and drink of Jesus Christ "renders those by whom it is taken, immortal and incorruptible, that is, the very fellowship of the saints, where will be peace and unity, full and perfect." Jesus Christ pointed our minds toward his body and blood, "in those things, which from being many are reduced to some one thing." Many grains, one bread; many grapes, one wine.

If we eat his body and drink his blood, we dwell in each other. However, if we do not live in Christ, we eat and drink to our ruin. "We are made better by the participation of the Son in the Father through the unity of his body and blood, which thing that eating and drinking signifies."

We live, then, by eating him, that is, by receiving him as the eternal life, which we do not have from ourselves. Sent by the Father, he lives by the Father. Augustine interprets Jesus' words, "As the living Father sent me, and I live by the Father—so he that eats me, even he shall live by me."

Sent by the Father, Jesus Christ lives by the Father, referring his life to the Father. So in order to live by Christ, we must participate in him by eating his flesh and blood. Though we participate in Christ through the eucharist, this is not the same way that Christ participates in his Father. However, Christ mediates for us to the Father, giving us eternal life.

Proof that we have eaten and drunk the body and blood of Christ is our mutual indwelling (*On John* 27). So Christ taught us,

> that we may be in his body, in his members, under himself as head, eating his flesh and not abandoning our unity with him.

However, most do not accept this because they are carnal minded.

We eat not the flesh and blood of Christ merely in the sacrament—but that we eat and drink to the participation of the spirit, that we abide as members of the Lord's body, to be quickened by his Spirit.

Jesus said that his bread is superior to Moses' manna. "For the true bread is he that comes down from heaven and gives life to the world." "Labor not for the meat which perishes, but for that which endures to eternal life." The manna was a sign of the true bread to come. Jesus said, "My Father gives you true bread," which comes down from heaven and gives life to the world.

Jesus told the Samaritan woman: "Whoever drinks of this water, will never be thirsty." But she thought that he meant the cool quaff from the well. Like those who ask for unfailing loaves of home-baked bread.

Jesus Christ is our bread of life. "He who comes to me will never hunger, and he who believes in me will never thirst." This is an eternal sufficiency in which there is no want.

Jesus also gave the dipped bread to Judas before he betrayed him. Was this the body of Christ? This was a warning that we should not receive the body of the Lord unworthily. "The point of special interest is not the thing received, but the person who receives it." For good things can be hurtful and evil things beneficial according to the character of the recipient. For example, if it is wrongly received (*On John* 62, 1).

Whosoever eats and drinks the bread and wine of the Lord unworthily, is guilty of the body and blood of the Lord (see 1 Cor 11:27). Thus one who eats the body of Christ carelessly, like a quick snack, comes to the table as a friend, but in reality is an enemy of Christ. So Satan entered into Judas fully after he had eaten the bread of the Lord unworthily. Beforehand Satan had been in Judas partially in order to tempt him. For Judas had already received the body and blood of Christ before the dipping (see Lk 22:19-21). The Lord, the living bread, gave this bread to the dead, revealing the betrayer of the bread.

Drinking the blood of the Lord is a spiritual experience, imbibing from the spiritual rock which is Christ (see 1 Cor 10:1-4) (*On John* 45, 9). When we dine at the ruler's table, we should consider wisely what is put before us (see Prv 33:1-2). "What is the table of the ruler but that from which we take the body and blood of him who laid down his life for us?" So we approach with humility (*On John* 84, 1).

Christ laid down his life for us, so we should do likewise for our brethren, following the example of the blessed martyrs, whose memories we celebrate "in the banquet whereat they themselves were filled to the full. To approach the table of the Lord, in their example, we must make similar preparations."

Rather than we pray for the martyrs, they should pray for us so that we can follow their example, since they have attained the fullness of love. "For such tokens of love they exhibited for their brethren, as they themselves had equally received at the table of the Lord."

The Christians of Carthage called baptism "Salvation" and the sacrament of the body and blood of Christ "Life." For without these two sacraments it is not possible to attain the kingdom of God, salvation or eternal life (see Jn 6:51-53) (*On the Forgiveness of Sin and Baptism* 1, 34).

If, therefore, as so many and such divine witnesses agree, neither salvation nor eternal life can be hoped for by any man without baptism and the Lord's body and blood, it is vain to promise these blessings to infants without them.

But do these sacraments also remove the guilt of sin from infants (see Job 14:4; Ps 51:5)? Christ died also for babies (*Against the Two Letters of the Pelagians* 1, 40; 2, 7)!

A frequent question from Augustine's congregation. How often should we receive the eucharist? Some say infrequently because of our sinfulness, lest we receive unworthily (L 54), while others counter, "If the wound of sin and the onset of disease are so great that such remedies are to be postponed," then all should be kept from the altar until they do penance.

However, "if his sins are not so great that one is judged fit for excommunication, he ought not to cut himself off from the daily remedy of the Lord's body." "Let each one do what he thinks he ought to do according to his faith and devotion," not to dishonor the body and blood of Christ, but to honor "this life-giving sacrament." Both Zacchaeus and the Centurion were sinners, but found mercy (see Lk 19:6; Mt 8:8).

Like the manna which tasted different to each one, "so in the heart of each Christian is the sacrament by which the world is brought into subjection." Thus some honor Christ by infrequent reception of the eucharist, others by frequent communion. "But that food is not to be despised as manna was not to be disliked." So the apostle warns against eating and drinking the body and blood of Christ like any other food (see 1 Cor 11:29).

> We respect the eucharist by our fasting. From this time it has pleased the Holy Spirit that, in honor of so great a sacrament, no other food should enter the mouth of a Christian before the Lord's body.

This is a worldwide custom, even though the Lord gave his body and blood to his apostles right after they had supped (see Mt 26:26). While Jesus recommended a special sublimity to his commemoration, he left its administration up to his followers.

But what of those who have committed grave sins after their baptism? How are they to be healed before receiving the eucharist?

Penance[1]

All Augustine's sins were wiped away by the cleansing waters of his

---

1. This section first appeared in *The Priest*, October 1991, 51-54.

baptism by Ambrose in Milan in 387. But what about post-baptismal faults? He discusses this important matter in his Sermons 351 and 352 (P) on the usefulness of penance.

Augustine teaches a threefold penance, the first of which is in baptism, which is clear from scriptures and Christian tradition.

Second penance is daily prayer, especially the Our Father, fasting and alms. Since we are in our weak flesh and so inclined to sin venially we should express our sorrow always. All venial sins should be recalled, that is, those which do not strike us a lethal blow, for example, murder, adultery and apostasy (S 351).

Gather up your small sins like so many itchy scabs. For if they are many, they can harm us unless they are dried up by the medicine of daily penance. We should confess daily lest with a stiff neck we merit the damnation of our arrogance (see 1 Jn 1:8; 3:9).

As a good son he receives from the dispenser of the sacraments the mode of his satisfaction. So that he does not only what is necessary for his own reparation, but also gives good example to others. For if his sin is not only grave, but also gives scandal, the bishop gives a condign penance.

Many Christians are too quick to give sinners the plus sign since it is so difficult to prove anything in the ecclesiastical courts. "For we cannot keep someone from communion (even though this is a medicinal prohibition) unless he spontaneously confesses, or either in a secular or church court he is indicted and convicted." Who would dare to be both prosecutor and judge? Paul gave the proper form for Church judgment (see 1 Cor 5:9-13).

Paul does not want anyone to be judged only on suspicion or by a tentative decision (see Rom 14:4), "but rather by the law of God according to Church order, either spontaneously confessed or accused and corrected."

Let no sinner despair, but fly to penance which is a change of life and satisfaction for sins. However, if you despair of healing, you add sins on top of your sins (see Prv 18:3; Ps 129:1-4).

Merciful Physician

Where can I flee from God's Spirit? Though we have contemned his power by our sins, there is no place to go except to his mercy in our repentance. We cannot escape to any place where his presence will not find us. Even if we do not do much to help our recovery, God accepts us anyway. "Why are you ignorant that God's patience leads you to repentance?" (Rom 2:4). He who cries out lest you fall away also calls for your return.

David, adulterer and murderer, from the depths of his crimes asked the Lord for forgiveness. For God does not spurn a contrite and humble heart (see Ps 50). It is not enough to have an interior change of heart. No, it must be shown through our sadness of repentance, groans of humility, our sacrifice of a contrite heart and alms, as Peter did.

"The keys of the Church are more certain than the hearts of kings. Because whatever is loosed on earth is loosed in heaven" (Mt 16:19). Humility is more honest by which we humble ourselves to the Church of God and a small work is imposed. So at no risk of temporal death eternal death is avoided.

The third type of penance, then, is graver and more sorrowful (S 352). In this stage they are properly called penitents and are removed from communion. This sad penance is concerned with a grave wound, for example, adultery, murder or sacrilege. Nevertheless, the divine physician is always ready to heal.

Although Lazarus was already in his tomb for four days and smelling, the Lord called him up from death to life. He was bound as are those who are doing penance, for they are proceeding from death to life. To confess is to climb from the dark depths up into the light (see Mt 18:18). As he did for Lazarus, the Lord fills the sinner with the good of his mercy, leading him to confession. The ministry of the Church does the rest (see Jn 11:39-44).

Pagans and heretics often insult Christians about their ecclesiastical penance. For example, some say that certain sins are too grave to submit to penance. Others say that by our practice of repentance we promote sin, for we promise them grace if they are sorry. However, we respond that if we close the door to repentance, "would not the sinner add further sins to his sins insofar as he despairs of forgiveness?" For he says to himself:

I have sinned and I admit my crime. But there is no place for grace or pardon for me. Repentance is fruitless. Since I am already damned, why shouldn't I do whatever I want? Since I will not find charity there, at least here and now I may enjoy my lust. So why should I abstain?

However, it is necessary that fear be in their minds in order that those who wish to avoid sin believe that God is present to them in public and private, day and night, outside and in, bedroom and heart. "Therefore, if you remove the door of repentance—in desperation sins multiply." Repentance does not cause loose morals, for we can never be sure that we will have time for repentance in the future.

God's providence guards us from despair and presumption. "Lest in despair we increase our sins he gives us the door of penance. And lest in hope we increase our faults, he gives us the uncertain day of death."

Grave sins require heavy penance (S 278) (P), while many light offenses tend to oppress us unless they are forgiven by God. Mortal sins committed after conversion are cleansed through serious humility of the heart, contrition of spirit and penance by the keys of the Church.

If we judge ourselves severely and become dissatisfied, God will come in his mercy. While we are punishing ourselves, he will spare us. Augustine comments, "If you perceive (*agnoscis*) your own sins, God forgives them (*ignoscit*)."

A multitude of small sins tends to press us down, as tons of wheat are collected from small grains until they overload a ship, putting it in danger of sinking. However, God forgives these lesser faults in us, if we pardon the mistakes of others.

In his *Enchiridion*,[1] Augustine further discusses some questions connected with our sin and repentance. Even if baptism removes all previous sins, the rest of our life, beginning with the use of reason, provides many occasions for the remission of sin.

Though they are sons of God and led by the Spirit, they are also sons of men in corruptible bodies. And "under the influence of human affections they fall back to the old level of sin."

Though it is possible through prayer and a holy life to live without crime, we cannot continue long without sin. However, even great crimes can be remitted through the Church and the mercy of God is never to be despaired of by those who truly repent.

Moreover, if a crime is committed which separates us from the body of Christ, "we are not to take account so much of the measure of time as of the measure of sorrow" (Ps 51:17). In order that the grief over our sins may be shown, the Church appoints certain times of repentance. For the Church has received the power to remit sins from the Holy Spirit (65).

Augustine notes (70) that grave sins cannot be atoned for by alms alone without a serious change of life. The Lord's Prayer takes away our smaller daily faults, repairing past wickedness which is duly repented, provided that we forgive others (71).

Alms means not only money, but also "applies to every useful act that a person does in mercy." For example, feeding the hungry, visiting the sick, advising the anxious, correcting and forgiving sinners, "not only in that he forgives, or prays for the forgiveness for the sin, but also in that he rebukes and corrects the sinner" (72). The greatest alms is to forgive those who sin against us and to love our enemies. For if we do not forgive others, God will not pardon us.

God decides between serious and trivial sins. Is it a sin to have intercourse with one's spouse without intending offspring? Or is it a sin to take Christian disputes to the civil courts (see 1 Cor 7:6)? "It is manifest that here again an indulgence is extended to the infirmities of the weak." For these things and other more trifling offenses in word and thought we need to pray daily the Our Father (78).

Sins that at first glance seem to be trivial, can be serious (79). For example, calling our brother a fool, or superstitions about days and times.

---

1. *Enchiridion*, ed. H. Paolucci, tr. J. Shaw (Chicago: Regnery, 1965). Next few quotes are from here.

On the other hand, grave sins can seem to be slight when we do them all the time (80). So many serious faults are openly practiced, "that not only dare we not excommunicate a layman, we dare not even degrade a clergyman for the commission of them." When we first see a heinous sin, we are shocked. However, "constant familiarity leads to the toleration of them all; and habitual toleration leads to the practice of many of them."

Augustine sees two main causes of sin: ignorance and weakness (81). For if we sin with full knowledge, we also transgress the law. "We leave undone what we know we ought to do," and do what we should not do. So we should pray for pardon and guidance against ignorance and weakness.

Penance is often avoided for reasons of infirmity (82). God's mercy leads to repentance and anyone who despises this can hardly be forgiven (83).

Augustine, like many of the Fathers in Judaeo/Christian tradition, is strongly pro-life. For example, he believes that aborted infants have really lived and died and so will rise again with Christ on the last day, when all deformities will be perfected. "At what time the infant begins to live in the womb: whether life exists in a latent form before it manifests itself in the motions of a living being."

> Now from the time that a man begins to live, from that time it is possible for him to die. And if he dies, wheresoever death may overtake him, I cannot discover on what principle he can be denied an interest in the resurrection of the dead. (86)

Even monstrosities will be restored to normal shape in the final resurrection (87).[1]

How often did people receive penance in Augustine's church? As Portalié notes,[2] Augustine himself probably did not receive it from the time of his baptism till his death, while his frequent prayers atoned for his daily faults.

Medicinal Lord's Prayer

From earliest Christianity, the faithful recited the Lord's Prayer, or the "Working man's Tephillah," a shortened form of the Jewish Eighteen Benedictions, three times a day, third, sixth and ninth hours. We will see how frequently Augustine endorses this basic Judaeo/Christian prayer.

> God established in the Church at the time of begging mercy a daily medicine, so that we say: "Forgive us our debts as we forgive our

---

1. Augustine discusses infant baptism in L 166; L 64; *On the Forgiveness of Sin and Baptism, Against Julian.* See p. 102
2. Portalié, *Guide,* 262.

debtors." So that by these words, with a clean face, we proceed to the altar, to receive the body and blood of Christ. (S 17)

We should never spurn this healthy medicine for our sins. Temptation comes, anger creeps up, our heart is troubled and our tongues spew out contentions and crimes. In order to correct these, we should say: "I have done evil; I sinned."

Augustine adds, "Believe not me, but God. What am I? I am but a man; I am your equal; I have flesh and I am weak. Let us all believe in God."

Augustine includes himself among the sinners. "I do not injure myself when I say that we bishops are also sinners" (S 56) (see 1 Jn 1:8). In our daily lives we commit sins which are daily remitted. Bilge has to be pumped out continually lest the ship sink. To pray is to pump out our faults. Moreover, we should not only pray, but also give alms. Small sins should not be contemned because they are so frequent. For we would be in bad shape if the daily cleansing of the holy prayer had not been given to us by our Lord and Savior, Jesus Christ.

Augustine urges his flock to abstain from idolatry, sorcery, heresy, schism, murder, adultery, fornication, stealing, rape, false testimony and other sins. Though venial sins are atoned for by alms and prayer, mortals must be submitted to the keys.

Portalié[1] believes that not all serious sins were subject to public penance (*On Faith and Works* 26, 48). However, certain sins merit excommunication as the apostle teaches (see 1 Cor 5:4-5; 2 Cor 12:21). Unless there were some sins not healed by the humility of penance such as given to the penitents in the Church, but by certain correcting medicines, the Lord would not have said (Mt 18:15): "Correct him between you and him alone. If he listens to you, you have gained a brother." Portalié remarks,[2] "Whatever meaning one wishes to attach to these remedies and this ecclesiastical correction, it is certain that there is a question of mortal sin."

Serious Public Sin and Public Penance

It seems that notorious public scandals are subject to public penance (S 351), according to the judgment of the bishop. Moreover, anyone who commits a serious sin should confess it and the bishop will decide an appropriate penance. After due penance, which in the case of grevious crimes included excommunication, the sinner is reconciled by the bishop or a delegated priest.

Augustine, like other Fathers, teaches that solemn penance cannot be

---

1. Portalié, *Guide*, 263-64.
2. Portalié, *Guide*, 264.

repeated, lest penance prove to be a cheap medicine. It seems that the relapsed could not receive communion until death, though, of course, God forgives them. This is the paradox of ecclesiastical penance from the beginning. If the Church makes it too easy, people will sin more readily. However, if she makes it too hard, they will sin even more in their despair of forgiveness. Though the rabbinical Pharisaic tradition of Paul seems harsh, the prophetic thrust of Jesus teaches compassion. The latter seems to be predominant in the Coptic monastic confession, while the former may be seen in the formal ecclesiastical courts.

In the time of Augustine very serious public sins are to be corrected publicly. Often it is difficult to find out precisely what they are. Judaeo/Christian tradition seems to limit them to murder, adultery and apostasy or idolatry.

Can we summarize the practice of penance around the time of Augustine? His threefold penance seems to be the norm. After baptism lesser sins are pardoned through daily charity or prayers such as the Our Father, while serious faults are confessed to the Church. It would seem that mistakes due to ignorance or weakness are not serious. But those done out of premeditation and malice should be submitted to the keys, and if public, public penance should be made. Serious sins confessed to the bishop or his representative, are atoned for by penance performed in the order of penitents for a prescribed period. Reconciliation and reception of communion is usually on Holy Thursday.[1]

In this chapter we have discussed several important sacraments as celebrated in Augustine's church, namely, baptism, the body and blood of the Lord and penance. Anointing usually accompanied baptism. Other sacraments we have seen earlier.[2] As Christ is God incarnate and his Church is his mystical body, so the sacraments are also incarnational, including the visible actions and the invisible mystery.

Besides the sacraments, prayer is another important pillar in Augustine's relationship with God and his divine Son. We will see more of Augustine's theology of prayer in the following chapter.

---

1. We discussed the *episcopalis audentia* on p. 85, note 1.
2. We discussed marriage in *Late Have I Loved You*, chap. 5 and ministry in this volume, chap. 5.

VIII.

YOU ARE MY GOD
AND I SIGH FOR YOU DAY AND NIGHT

(*Confessions* 7, 10)[1]

The Mystic Stream

Mysticism comes from the Greek word *musticos*, pertaining to the mysteries or secret rites. Dionysius uses it to describe the direct contemplation of God.

The mystics, like the gnostics before them, claim to experience divine union, but it is difficult to explain. It seems to be a free, unearned gift of God, who can reveal himself to whomever he wishes and who can give human beings the capacity for receiving this gift.

Many mystics insist that God is really within us all the time and all we have to do is stop our hectic busyness and stifle the darkness of passion and the divine light will shine through. But in our deepest contemplation we meet the black night of divine incomprehensibility.

Is the mystic experience common or rare? Some maintain that God grants this charism only occasionally to specially chosen saints, while others assert that close divine union is within the reach of many. The mystic tradition is found in most religions and cultures from Hinduism to Christianity.

Plato and Plotinus and the Ascent to the One

Plato taught that the soul is drawn upwards by the divine Eros, leading it toward true Beauty. And when a person dies, his or her soul ascends to the Good. "Since it (the soul) is always practicing this—here we have nothing else but a soul loving wisdom rightly, and in reality practicing death" (*Phaedo* 81a). Freed from the vagaries and changeableness of the body, the soul enjoys the peace and tranquility of divine union.

Pieper remarks on Plato's *Phaedrus*:[2] Love, insofar as it is a real ekstasis,

---

1. This essay first appeared in *Emmanuel*, April 1991.
2. *Love and Inspiration* (London: Faber and Faber, 1964), 89.

a steppingstone outside of the narrow circle of the self-enclosed ego, a frenzy or mania, is capable of carrying aloft with it the heaviest burden, for it remembers the holy things that it once contemplated.

Platonism found a home in Alexandria under the leadership of men like Philo and Plotinus. Like Plato, Plotinus teaches a return to the transcendent One. The goal is the starting point; the image reflects and is drawn to its archetype in which its perfection lies. However, before the soul can ascend, it must first separate itself from the multiplicity of matter and leave off discursive reason.

Since the soul is the image of God, "true knowledge of self and true knowledge of God are so intimately linked within the soul that if the soul is purified of all that is not itself, it knows at one and the same time itself and in itself God."[1]

Plotinus compares the mystical experience to someone so absorbed in reading that he is unaware that he is reading. There is no longer a subject-object dichotomy for he or she is inside the object and the divine light replaces the dualism of discursive knowledge.

Those who are too weak for contemplation try to seek its shadow in action. But contemplation must precede action because action is a derivation of and a weaker form of contemplation (*Enneads* 3, 8, 5). "All proceeds silently. The soul needs no visible or external object for contemplation and it engages in no action. It is soul. It contemplates." The soul desires contemplation, channeling its actions in this direction. So contemplation is the end of its action.

One desires an object as it is possessed and contemplated within his soul. "Through action the soul comes back to contemplation" (6). The soul "is sated, its vision remains all within; it is sure of its object. The greater this assurance the more tranquil is the contemplation and the more unified the soul. Knower and known are one" (6).

"The soul is richer in content than nature is and so it is more at rest and more contemplative." Contemplation rises from Nature to the Soul to Intelligence in which knower and known are one. But there is still multiplicity because of the multiple objects.

He who contemplates the Intelligence, enters in and becomes one with it. "So the contemplative who has gazed upon the intelligible realm and been struck with the wonder of it should seek out its author," the Good (11).

Plotinus' search for union with the Good and the One, reversing the divine emanation, leaps into ecstasy. His teachings would influence Gregory of Nyssa, Augustine, Dionysius and other mystics.

---

1. E. O'Brien, tr., *The Essential Plotinus* (Toronto: New American Library, 1964), 29.

Augustine's Interior Path

The young Augustine was introduced to Plotinus' teaching in Rome. And his early writings reflect the Neoplatonic interior path to God through his image in the soul, where the divine Beauty is mirrored in us.

In his *Soliloquies* (F), written at Cassiciacum while awaiting baptism, Augustine dialogues with his reason who advises him to write out his prayer in order to help himself and others.

> O God, the Founder of the Universe, grant me first of all that I may fittingly supplicate you; next, that I may so act that I may be worthy of a hearing from you; finally, I beg you to set me free.

Augustine calls on God, Truth, Wisdom, Beauty, Good. To turn away from him means falling and death. Only through God can we overcome the enemy, do good, flee evil, etc.

"Hear me, O hear me in that way of yours well known to a selected few." Him alone Augustine loves, follows, seeks, senses and obeys. "Let your door be open to my knocking. Teach me how to come to you." He asks only that God convert him wholly to himself (1).

Augustine's *Confessions*[1] relate his long search for God. As a young man he enjoyed lesser beauties. But Cicero's Hortensius spurred his upward flight to Beauty.

Under God's guidance, Augustine enters into his inmost being. "I entered there, and by my soul's eye, such as it was, I saw above my mind, an unchangeable light" (7, 10). This is the light which made him. "He who knows the truth, knows that light, and he who knows it, knows eternity. You are my God, and I sigh for you day and night."

When Augustine first knows God, he is lifted up. But still not able to see, he hears God's voice from afar. "You will be changed into me." "I am who am." He hears these words in his heart without a doubt. "It is good for me to adhere to my God. For if I do not abide in him, neither will I be able to abide in myself" (7, 11).

Though he is borne up to God by his divine beauty, yet he is also pulled down by the weight of inferior things. "Still there remains within me a remembrance of you. I did not doubt in any way that there was one to cleave to, nor did I doubt that I was not yet one who would cleave to him" (7, 17).

Augustine passes from bodies to the soul, then to its inferior power, then to reason, to understanding, withdrawing his thoughts from habit and phantasm. "In this way I might find that light by which it was sprinkled," and know the immutable. But the invisible strikes him back, leaving him with a memory and a longing for what he had.

Like Plato, Plotinus and others, Augustine had been attracted by earthly

---

1. *Confessions*, tr. J. Ryan (Garden City: Doubleday, 1960). Next few quotes are from here.

beauties. But God cries out to him, shining his divine light on him. And Augustine smells God's fragrance and tastes his delights. "You have touched me and I have burned for your peace" (10, 27).

Psalms

Augustine comments on Psalm 38 (N),[1] in which the psalmist cries with a groaning heart. Our heart's desire is our prayer. And if our desire is uninterrupted, our prayer is continuous as well.

> Whatever else you are doing, if you but long for the Sabbath, you do not cease to pray. If you would never cease to pray, never cease to long for it. The continuance of your longing is the continuance of your prayer. (13)

Psalm 41. "My soul is athirst for the living God," as the heart yearns for the cool, living waters. "I am athirst in my pilgrimage, in my running. And I shall be filled on my arrival." He has only one desire—to dwell in the house of the Lord (2).

"I thought on these things and poured out my soul above myself" (4). If my soul rests in itself, it will not see anything beyond itself. "And, in seeing itself, would not, for all that, see God." "I have poured forth my soul above myself, and there remains no longer any being for me to attain to, save my God.

The heart leaps toward the tabernacle of God, "led on by the sweetness of that inward spiritual sound to feel contempt for all outward things and to be borne on to spiritual things." But he is still a mortal man, groaning in the midst of the world and hoping for the delights of the refreshing fountain (4).

Psalm 44. Alms and fasting give wings to prayer. "Fast on account of your prayers, that you may be heard in them." While we are yet speaking, he will say, "I am here," if we cheerfully break bread with the hungry. "How speedily are the prayers of the just received, who work righteousness." "Would you have your prayers fly upwards to God?" Use your wings of alms and fasting (7).

Psalm 66. If I hold no iniquity in my heart, God will hear my prayer. We pray that God will not cast away our supplication and will show us his mercy, "that we may pray continually and he continually pity."

Though many pray fervently in the beginning, they soon grow negligent, feeble, cold and sure of themselves. But the foe watches even while we sleep. The gospel says to pray always and not to grow faint (see Lk 18:1). Though God may put off granting our wish, he does not put it away and forget it.

---

1. Next few quotes are from here.

"Being secure of his promise, let us not be faint in praying. And this is by his goodness" (2).

Psalm 86. When we speak to God in prayer, we should not separate his Son from him. "When the body of the Son prays, it separates not its head from itself." The Savior of his body, our Lord, Jesus Christ, the Son of God, prays for us and prays in us, and is prayed to by us. He prays for us as our priest, in us as our head, and is prayed to as God.

As God he is prayed to; as the servant of God, he prays, assuming creaturehood and making us one with him. "Therefore, we pray to him, through him and in him; and we speak with him and he speaks with us" (1).

Sermon on the Mount and the Lord's Prayer

In his *Commentary on the Sermon on the Mount* (F) he warns not to pray like hypocrites—to please people (3, 10) (see Mt 6:5-8). Rather pray in the bedroom of the heart, with the doors closed against outside distractions. "This prayer is formed in the depth of the heart, where one prays in secret to the Father."

To petition God we should plead our cause, not by words, but by "the truths which we cherish in our mind and by the application of thought with pure love and single affection." But if God is all-knowing, why pray? "The very attention of our prayer clears and cleanses our heart, and makes it more capable of receiving the divine gifts which are spiritually infused into us" (14). Through our prayer and change of heart we are readily turned to the divine light.

Augustine, following ancient Christian Tradition, teaches the Our Father as the epitome of prayer. From earliest Christianity, the faithful recited the Lord's Prayer, or the "Workingman's Tephillah," a shortened form of the Jewish Eighteen Benedictions, three times a day, at the third, sixth and ninth hours. Frequently Augustine endorses this basic Judaeo-Christian orison.

We begin the Lord's Prayer with our praise of the Father from his adopted sons and daughters, coheirs with Christ. By calling him Our Father, our love is enkindled and our confidence restored. For, even before we ask, we already have the privilege of addressing him as Father. What more do we desire, if we are already God's children? Our family pride should prohibit us from doing anything unworthy of our brothers and sisters in the Lord.

Augustine notes that the seven petitions of the Lord's Prayer parallel the beatitudes with similar virtues and rewards. Moreover, he recommends the Our Father as a means of asking forgiveness for our lesser sins, provided that we excuse others, as we have seen (S 17). Thus in the liturgy the purifying Lord's Prayer precedes our reception of the body and blood of the Lord.

Even the best of us make daily mistakes. We lose our tempers, make uncharitable remarks, etc. So the best approach to healing is to admit our weaknesses. Augustine includes himself among the sinners, as we have seen (S 56). So he along with his congregation recite the curative Tephillah of Jesus.

Contemplation in Action

In his *The Trinity* (8, 10) Augustine identifies the worship of God with the love of him. Our very mind reflects God's triune nature. Thus memory, intellect and will not only remember, know and love the self, "but because it [the mind] can also remember, understand and love him by whom it was made . . . let it remember its God to whose image it has been made, and understand and love him" (14, 12) (F).

In his *The City of God*[1] Augustine makes the classical distinction among the three modes of life: contemplative, active and contemplative/active. All three are good, if one loves the truth and does charity.

"No man must be so committed to contemplation as, in his contemplation, to give no thought to his neighbor's needs, nor so absorbed in action as to dispense with the contemplation of God" (19, 19).

Our leisure should not lead us into indolence and our activity ought to help others to salvation. Reflecting his own experience in the ministry, Augustine notes that if no burden of charity, such as a bishopric, is placed on our shoulders, "time should be passed in study and contemplation." But a bishop should never give up his contemplation, lest his burden overwhelm him.

Is contemplation of God something only available to the super-intellectuals? As a pastor, Augustine is concerned with the little ones who follow the cross of Christ, "who perseveringly walk in the road of faith and come to that blessed contemplation." Others may have more knowledge, but still refuse to follow the way of the cross (L 120).

Letter to Widow Proba

The widow Proba, exiled in Africa, asks Augustine's advice on prayer. He replies that nothing is more important for a widow than praying day and night. Moreover, he is happy that God has inspired her with a devout anxiety about prayer (L 130) (F).

Though wealthy and surrounded by her devoted family, Proba is, nevertheless, depressed, for she knows that these gifts will pass. So she prays continually for lasting happiness and peace.

---

1. *The City of God*, tr. G. Walsh et al. (Garden City: Doubleday, 1953).

True Life, Christ, taught us how to attain this blessed life and not to be wordy, for the Lord knows our needs (see Mt 6:7-8). Yet the persistent widow kept bothering the sleeping judge until he finally got out of bed to answer the door. How much more readily will God answer us, for he never sleeps.

Ask and receive. Though God knows our needs before we ask, "he wishes our desire to be exercised in prayer that we may be able to receive what he is preparing to give us."

> Desire and pray. But because that desire grows somewhat lukewarm by reason of our cares and preoccupation with other things, we call our mind back to the duty of praying at fixed hours.

Our desires are made known not to God, but to us before God through our patience, or made known to the angels who intercede for us.

It is not useless to pray at length as long as it does not interfere with other obligations, however, we should not be too wordy. "Continual longing is not the same as much speaking." The Lord himself spent the whole night in prayer.

The Egyptian monks sent up brief prayers like arrows shot up to heaven, "so that the alert attention, necessary in prayer, does not fade out and grow heavy through long drawn-out periods." "Prayer is to be free of much speaking, but not of much entreaty, if the fervor and attention persist." Entreating is "to knock by a long-continued and devout uplifting of the heart," with sighs and tears.

Words are more necessary to wake *us* up than to arouse God. For example, "Your kingdom come," lifts up our desire for the kingdom. Also "our daily bread" and "deliver us from evil," beginning and ending with tears.

> We say nothing that is not found in the prayer of the Lord, if we pray properly and fittingly. Otherwise our prayer is carnal and perhaps should be forbidden. For, if we are reborn in the spirit, we should pray in a spiritual manner.

"If you were to run over all the words of holy prayers, you would find nothing . . . which is not contained in the Lord's Prayer." For example, we find no covetous or selfish petitions there. Faith, hope and charity "lead the praying soul to God, that is, the believing, hoping and desiring soul who attends to what he asks of the Lord in the Lord's Prayer." Fasting, abstinence and alms also help us to pray.

Often we pray that our trials will go away. In the Bible many prayers were heard, even those of the devil (see Job 1:12, Mt 8:30-32). So we should not think well of ourselves if our prayer is heard, and not despair of divine mercy, if our request is not answered. Sometimes we do not know what we should pray for. We should ask for what God wants and not for what we covet. Both God and we desire eternal life.

Though we may not know what to pray for, the Holy Spirit asks for us with unspeakable cries (see Rom 8:25, 27). The Lord makes the saints ask with groanings, "breathing into them the desire of this great thing, as yet unknown, which we await in patience."

Strive in prayer to overcome the world in faith, hope and love. Moreover, pray insistently and submissively like the widow in the parable. The Bible portrays widows as women of prayer. Even though Proba is blessed with much wealth and a loving family, she should pray as if poor and desolate.

"Vie with each other in prayer in a mutual and holy rivalry, for you will not vie against each other, but against the devil, who is the enemy of all saints." Also do what you can in fasting, watching and chastisement.

As we have seen, Augustine follows the popular Neoplatonic ascent to God, leading from the knowledge of beautiful creatures to the wisdom of the contemplation of divine Beauty. Although by nature introspective and philosophical, Augustine accepts the bishopric of Hippo out of duty and charity, at the same time living in a religious community. His prayerful insights are handed on in his sermons, letters and other works.

Inspired by God's graces, Augustine prays with a vision and a hope for eternal life. Thus, in a sense, God rewards his own gifts. We will discuss Augustine's theology of hope in the following chapter.

IX.

HOPE HAS FOR ITS OBJECT ONLY WHAT IS GOOD

(*Enchiridion* 8)

Augustine's theology of hope is based solidly on sacred scriptures, beginning with the Hebrew Bible's trust in Yahweh who cannot deceive in lieu of his undependable creatures.

Psalms of Hope

Psalm 9 (N). "Let them who know your name, hope in you." Augustine comments:

> And when they shall have ceased hoping in wealth and other entice-ments of the world. For the soul, indeed, that seeks where to fix her hope, when she is torn away from this world, the knowledge of God's name she seasonably receives.

"Let them who know your name, hope in you," and not hope in transient worldly things. For we eagerly wait for earthly pleasures which we promptly and painfully lose.

However, in God nothing is future or past, for all is eternal. "Let them cease then to hope in and love temporal things and let them apply themselves to hope eternal."

Augustine remarks on Psalm 40:

> Let the Lord, your God, be your hope and hope for nothing else from the Lord, your God. But rather let the Lord, your God, be your hope. For many hope to obtain from the Lord's hands wealth and many perishable honors, and, in short, anything else they hope to obtain from God except the Lord himself.

So forget worldly things and remember the eternal God. "Let him, then, be your hope, who both guides you and leads you to your destination."

Psalm 130. "Lord hear my voice." When the sinner cries out to God, what does he or she hope for? "Because he who came to absolve our sins gave hope to sinners down in the depths." Why is there hope? "Because there is propitiation with you," through Christ's innocent sacrifice.

We trust in God, who cannot deceive us. "My soul trusted in the Lord from the morning watch even unto night" (Ps 130). Our Lord, who removed our sins, rose from the dead at the early morning watch. "So that we may hope that what went before in the Lord will also take place in us."

Our head, who rose before us, said: "What you have seen in me, hope for in yourselves. Because I have risen from the dead, you also shall rise again." Why should we base our hopes on Christ's resurrection? Because what rose was what he acquired from us, namely, his body.

Christ says to us: "All that is yours is now consecrated." Thus he offers our first fruits along with his. "Hope, therefore, that that will take place in yourself which went before in your first fruits." Since Christ rose at the morning watch, "our soul began to hope from that moment," even up until night comes when we sleep in death.

"From the morning watch let Israel hope" (Ps 130). But this is not an earthly hope for wealth, fame or health, since, like the Lord, we will have to suffer here below.

However, Christ rose from the dead because he was sinless. Where does that leave us sinners? Christ, our head, went before us sinless to die for our sins.

"I will sing unto the Lord in my life" (Ps 104). "Our life at present is only hope, but it will be eternity hereafter. Because the mortal life is the hope of an everlasting happiness."

Psalm 126. Though our lives are confused, the Lord comforts and consoles us. Consolation is for those who groan and mourn. So while we complain over our present lot, we are comforted in hope that our mourning will turn into joy.

Psalm 145. We have God's promise that he will reward our faith. Since he has given us so much already, he will also offer us what is still owed. "I promised that I would give by my Son earnest of the Holy Spirit."

"The eyes of all hope in you, and you give them food in due season" (Ps 145). Sometimes no matter how much we plead and cry God does not give us what we want. Augustine responds, "He who tends, knows the time to give." Remember that if our request is right we should not despair, but rather await the divine food which will be given in due season.

"The Lord is near to all who call upon him" (Ps 145). However, we must be honest in our request. Moreover, if we see how good God is for having given us all that we have, "how much more blessed will we be when he gives us himself?"

"He will hear our prayer and save us." The divine Physician listens to us in order to save us. Paul reminds us that we are saved in our hope (see Rom 8:24). However, once we possess the object of our desire, we will no longer need hope. But while it remains unseen, we have to wait patiently in anticipation.

The Lord will save all the faithful who hope in him, fear him and call upon him in truth. However, those who stubbornly argue against God and blame him despair of pardon for their sins or else they proudly forgive themselves, while they await their proper punishment.

Though we groan under the weight of life's problems, "our hope is in the Lord, our God" (Ps 146). While the pagans place their hopes in Saturn, Neptune and Mercury, our hope is in the Lord who made all creation.

If we admire the world, why not the maker of the world? For he made and cares for the universe and all that is in it. But how much better are we than animals and plants (see Mt 10:29)?

Sermons of Hope

Augustine preaches on the feast of the Nativity, a time of great hope (S 192) (F). On this festive day remember the eternal Day—desiring eternal gifts with an unfaltering hope, as inheriting children of God.

> A far brighter hope has now shone upon the earth as a pledge to mortal men of life in heaven. To gain credence in this guarantee an incredible event has been promised, that is God became human, died for our sins and rose again.

> Psalm 193. In proportion as we believe and hope and desire, we, too, shall be a source of additional glory to God in the highest when after the resurrection of our spiritual body we shall be lifted up in the clouds to meet Christ, provided we have worked for peace in good will.

On New Year's Day Augustine notes (S 197) that the Lord himself was born in a humble place and picked very ordinary people to be his disciples. So "let no lowly person despair. Rather let us hold fast to Christ and our hope will not go unrewarded." Augustine's audience in the Hippo cathedral included the wealthy and titled but also illiterate peasants.

Augustine agrees with Paul, namely, that the apostle plants, Apollos waters, but God gives the increase (see 1 Cor 3:7, 1:13). "The apostle wished the hope of his hearers to be centered not in himself, but in the truth he was presenting." For the divine message is more important than the human messenger. This also reflects Augustine's philosophy of education and preaching, as we have seen.

The whole of New Testament hope is based on the resurrection of Christ as illustrated in Augustine's Easter sermons. "Let your hope be not on earth but in heaven" (S 228). To the recently baptized he cautions:

> Now you are one of the faithful. So do not act sinfully. You have been

baptized; you are reborn. Your hopes have been changed; let your character also be changed.

As they partake of the one bread, the eucharist, "may you also be one body by loving one another, by having one faith, one hope and an undivided charity" (S 229).

The bishop often speaks of the two discouraged disciples who met Jesus on the road to Emmaus, though they did not recognize him (see Lk 24:17-22).

They had lost hope while we, on our part, have no doubt about what caused them to hesitate. For when their Lord was crucified, they lost hope. "But we were hoping," they said to the stranger (Jesus). You were hoping. Are you no longer hoping? Is this the extent of your discipleship? "We were hoping." What were you hoping? "That it was he who should redeem Israel." However, what you hoped for and then lost at the crucifixion, that a thief on the cross understood. (S 234)

Christ taught the good thief on Calvary's mount. So "let him who gave himself for you revive hope in you for so it was done there."

It is in the eucharist that the despairing disciples recognize their Lord.

You who hear the word of God with sentiments of fear and hope, let the breaking of bread bring consolation to you. For the absence of the Lord is not a real absence.

Have faith and he whom you do not see is with you. But when the Lord spoke to the disciples they did not have faith because they did not believe that he had risen. Moreover, they did not hope that they could rise again, for they had lost faith and hope.

As dead men they walked with Life. And though Life accompanied them on their journey, their souls were not vivified. Despite their moribund faith and hope, Christ lives!

S 236 (P). Pascal time. When Christ died, his followers quickly lost all hope. And even when his resurrection was announced to them, it all seemed like a foolish fantasy. Yet as the stranger on the way to Emmaus began to explain the scriptures how it was necessary for Christ to die in order to enter into his glory, their blind and depressed eyes began to see and hope (see Lk 24:13-31).

Augustine tells his flock that the happy days after Easter anticipate the joyful eternal life, following our own resurrection (S 243).

The life which is symbolized by the fifty days after Easter is not possessed now, but is an object of hope and is loved while it is hoped for. By that very love we praise God who promised this Eternal Life to us. And our praises are alleluias.

S 261. Ascension. "The resurrection of the Lord is our hope, while his ascension is our exaltation." We want to join in our Lord's ascension so our hearts are lifted up with his.

> He rose again to give us hope that what dies will rise again. Lest in dying we should despair and think that our whole life has come to an end.

As he came down to heal us, he ascended in order to lift us up. When the Lord rises, we should say, "Because you, O Lord, are my hope." And when he ascends, we cry out, "You have made the most high your refuge" (Ps 90).

S. 265. Ascension. After his resurrection Jesus Christ manifested himself alive to his disciples, "who had lost hope in him, as one dead." However, when he stayed with them for forty days until his ascension into heaven, they rejoiced. "For the precedence of the head is the hope of the members." Both they and we expect his second coming in hope.

> We longingly gaze upwards in expectancy and suspense, desiring to find out when the Lord, our God, is going to come. If I were able to tell you when, how great would I seem in your eyes.

Paul and John

Augustine bases his theology of hope solidly on these two apostles. For example, in his *Confessions* (13, 13-14), quoting Paul (see 2 Cor 5:7; Rom 8:24), Augustine notes that the object of both faith and hope is unseen, though enthusiastically anticipated (see 2 Cor 5:2-4).

Paul hopefully and patiently awaits the first fruits of the Spirit laid up by his union with Christ, while his soul expects the divine adoption (see Rom 8:23). Moreover, as a member of the Church, the bride of Christ, he hopes for the coming of his bridegroom.

S. 157 (P) (Chap. 1). Paul tells us that the hope of Christians rests in the unseen eternal (see Rom 8:24-25). However, if we already possess the object of our desire, what is left to hope for? On the other hand, if we do not see our prize, we should hope for it and patiently await its arrival.

"You are my hope, my portion in the land of the living" (Ps 141). He who is our hope in the land of the living rejoices that we address you in the land of the dead. So that you will not become enamored with visible things. For those things that are seen are temporal, while those that are invisible are eternal (see 2 Cor 4:18). Although worldly promises are illusions, God's are certain.

The world's promises never measure up to expectations, but God's do. Though the world's pledges sometimes seem to come true, what God guarantees we will definitely receive in the land of the living. However, some, tired of waiting for eternal life, fall for the fallacious. People laugh at Christians for hoping for something unseen, while they see and enjoy the object of their desires here and now.

Chap. 2. Patience and gentleness are the watchwords. So be careful lest your morals become corrupted and your hope be destroyed and your resolve weakened. For without patience our hope in a distant, invisible future life cannot be sustained. In all meekness we should believe, hope in and love God. "Because we do not see what we hope for, we await it with equanimity."

Chap. 3. We already see in our head, Christ, what we hope for. So we walk calmly in the Lord, while he strengthens us by the example of his resurrection. We are the body of his head in which that is already perfect that we hope for. "He who raised up our head serves our hope." Moreover, his prior passion and death strengthens our constancy in the midst of our trials.

Chap. 4. "No longer are we left without joy because we are saved by our hope." "Rejoicing in hope, we are patient in tribulation" (Rom 12:12). Why hope in eternal life which our earthly eyes cannot even glimpse? However, temporal desires often turn out for the worse, whereas what we hope for, once it comes will not disappear. Rather we use earthly things to help us toward the eternal.

Chap. 6. Our Christian hope is more certain than merely human wishes (see Jer 17:5). For when God became human, died and rose again, he showed us in his human flesh what we will achieve in ours.

Augustine also comments on John's gospel of hope (N), while he lifts his eyes to the mountain of hope (see Ps 120).

> It is not the mountains themselves in which our hope is to be placed. For the mountains receive what they may present to us. Therefore, we must put our hope in that place from which the mountains also receive the true light (see Jn 1:9).

Though John the Baptizer is a mountain, he is not the Christ (see Jn 1:20). "In order that no one, placing hope in the mountain, might fall from him who illuminates the mountain." "Of his fullness we have all received" (Jn 1:16) (*Commentary on John* 1, 6, 2-3) (N).

The Israelites placed all their hopes in one man, Moses. But when he died, it was God who led them out of the land of Egypt. And how quickly they forgot, turning rather to false gods (3, 10, 3).

Since Christ is our hope, we should not run to enchanters or fortune tellers for cures (7, 7, 4). "One who is sick, but has hope, is called healable. However, one who is already healthy does not need a physician (7, 18, 3).

Christ died and rose

> that he might show us the hope of the immortality of his Church. He showed in the head what the members ought to expect. For he who arose in the head will also arise in his members. (8, 12, 2)

Paul warns that we should never muzzle the ox who tramples the grain. "He says this for our sakes. For he who plows ought to plow in hope. And he who threshes should have hopes of partaking in the grain" (1 Cor 9:10) (10, 7, 1).

> Furthermore, we should not let our worldly success puff us up. Rather let our joy come from hope for the future. Let our desire be for eternal life. Let every sigh be a panting after Christ. Let that most beautiful one who loved even the ugly that he might make them beautiful, let him be longed for. (10, 13)
> However, if no one but Christ descended and ascended, what hope is there for the rest of us? There is the hope that he descended precisely in order that those who are going to ascend through him might be one in him and with him. (12, 9, 1)

What reward should we expect from all of our moral life? We look "for that blessed hope and revelation of the glory of the great God, our Savior, Jesus Christ." "In that hope, when reality shall have come to pass from hope, we shall receive a denarius, a wage" (17, 4, 3).

Enchiridion

Augustine's friend Laurentius asked him for a manual to help him answer questions posed by the Roman Christians. Augustine bases his work on the three theological virtues, faith, hope and love, explained through the Apostles Creed and the Lord's Prayer.

God is to be worshipped through his three graces, faith, hope and charity. While faith believes, hope and love pray.[1] Faith and hope are interrelated. Thus we cannot hope for something which is not the object of faith, though we can believe something that is not the object of hope.

"Hope has for its object only what is good, only what is future and only affects the hoper" (8). In this it is distinguished from faith. "But the fact that we do not see either what we believe or what we hope is all that is common to faith and hope."

As we have noted, Paul teaches the invisibility of the object of hope (see Rom 8:24-25). So we must await patiently its arrival. "When we believe that good is about to come, this is nothing else but to hope for it."

Love is the driving force behind faith and hope. Paul (see Gal 5:6) says that faith works through love. "And this certainly cannot exist without hope. Therefore, there is no love without hope, no hope without love and neither love nor hope without faith."

---

1. *Enchiridion*, tr. J. Shaw (Chicago: Regnery, 1961), 7. Next few quotes are from here.

From the Creed springs "the good hope of believers" and this is joined with love. Furthermore, "those only pertain to hope which are embraced in the Lord's Prayer" (114).

> Therefore, except from God the Lord we ought to ask for nothing either that we hope to do well, or hope to obtain as a reward for our good works.

Matthew's Lord's Prayer includes seven petitions, three pertaining to eternal life and four temporal requests, which aid us on our road to heaven.

> In that eternal life where we hope to live forever, the hallowing of God's name, his kingdom and his will in our spirit and body shall be brought to perfection and shall endure to everlasting. (115)

But while still on earth we ask for our daily bread, forgiveness and deliverance from evil.

> Love is greater than faith and hope. Why? When there is a question as to whether a person is good, one does not ask what one believes or what one hopes, but what he or she loves.

For the person who loves properly also believes and hopes rightly. For without love, our faith and hope are fruitless. Moreover, we believe and hope to obtain through our prayers the blessings of love.

> Although it is not possible to hope without love, it may yet happen that we do not love that which is necessary for the attainment of our hope,

that is, pursuing a righteous way to eternal life.

Augustine next describes the four main stages of life which can also be applied to the evolution of the Church (118). While the first phase is ignorance, the second is the law. But if we have faith and the Spirit of God with love, we live the life of the just by faith and live in righteousness, while we conquer lust by our love of holiness.

> This is the third state of a person of good hope and who by steadfast piety advances in this course shall attain at last to peace.

The fourth era is our final repose, the resurrection of the body, eternal life or paradise regained.

Paradise

Augustine's theology of creation and paradise complements his hopeful views of the earth and matter against the pessimistic Manichaeans. Though the beautiful Eden was lost by the first Adam, the new Adam, Christ, redeemed it giving us the graces to cultivate our interior paradise, filled with lovely trees and flowers of virtues.

The ultimate goal of our hopes is called paradise for it lies in the East where heaven begins. Moreover, Eden means to be filled with immortal and intelligible delights. The tree of life signifies wisdom, while the tree of knowledge signals moderation and integrity. The four-branched stream includes the cardinal virtues.

In Augustine's *Literal Interpretation of Genesis* (4) (P), Christ is the tree of life and the new Adam in a spiritual paradise. God not only creates the good earth, but also guides it by his twofold providence through nature and through his human and angelic voluntary helpers.

Augustine also speaks of the seminal reasons by which God both makes and perfects the world. Initially God created formless matter. However, when he says his Word, he turns matter toward himself, imitating the Word's adherence to his Father.

> As the Word is the perfect image of the Father by virtue of his complete adherence to him, so matter becomes an imperfect image of the Word and his ideas by turning toward him.

Thus God creates unformed matter, which he calls back to himself in form.[1]

Paradise, the origin and goal of Christian hope, can also be an allegory of the Church with the four gospels as the rivers and Christ as the tree of life, anticipating our final paradise of eternal life (*The City of God* 13, 21).

As creation called up form from the void, so Edenic reform continues the process. In his seminal reasons Augustine finds a paradigm of our own regeneration (22, 24). For in both natural and supernatural evolution God gives the increase (see 1 Cor 3:7). So our Church paradise prepares us along the road to heaven or paradise, the invisible goal of our Christian hope.

Conclusion

Augustine's theology of hope follows the lead of scriptures which advise us to place our trust in the Creator who cannot lie in lieu of his ephemeral creatures, hoping for the Messiah in the Old Law and for his second coming in the New, with our own resurrection anticipated by the victory of Christ, our head.

Augustine's *Enchiridion* sums up his theology of hope. For hope along with faith and love is a foundation stone of the Creed and the Lord's Prayer. Love is most important for without it faith and hope cannot survive. More-

---

1. See Gilson, *Christian Philosophy*, 205-09.

over, love alone remains once the divine object is possessed in eternal life or paradise, the unseen object of our hope.

Hope for our final peace in the city of God keeps us going along on our earthly journey. "Already in longing we are there. Already we are in hope into that land." Hope is our firm anchor lest we suffer shipwreck in our stormy voyage to the divine city (see Ps 65).

In the following and final chapter we will see Augustine's theology of the two cities, built on the two loves of creation and its Creator.

X.

TWO CITIES HAVE ISSUED
FROM TWO KINDS OF LOVE

(*The City of God* 14, 28)

Augustine's most cogent views on government and politics may be found in his *The City of God* (413-26). When he set out to write his epic of the good and the bad, the Roman Empire was collapsing due to the barbarian invasions from without and problems within. As Bourke mentions,[1] some of the old-line pagan families saw Christianity as a weakening influence on Rome. A Roman official and friend of Augustine, named Marcellinus alerted him of this accusation.

So in response to this false charge, Augustine began to write his *The City of God*, the first part of which refutes the pagans, while the second part defends the Christian religion.

The two cities of Augustine are based on the love of God and an earthly love. But Augustine is not proposing an ideal Christian kingdom like the Holy Roman Empire of later times. Rather the two societies are battling within us until we reach the final goal.

The two metropolises have biblical models in Jerusalem and Babylon and can be seen in Zoroastrian and intertestamental literature plus Augustine's contemporary, Tychonius. Moreover, since the Church contains people of both good and bad will, it cannot be contiguous with the city of God here on earth.

The People and the Good

Any city consists first of all of the people (*populus*).[2] Who are the people? Augustine quotes Scipio[3] that the commonwealth is the prosperity or the good

---

1. V. Bourke, *The Essential Augustine* (New York: Mentor-Omega, 1964), 197-98.
2. *Populus Romanus* included the whole citizenry of the Roman state, including both patricians and plebians, a collectivity of persons with its own rights and existence. See Berger, *Encyclopedic Dictionary*, 636 (B). Further references will refer to B.
3. *The City of God*, tr. G. Walsh et al. (Garden City: Doubleday, 1953), 2, 21, 73. *The City of God* quotes from here, unless otherwise noted. The battle between good and evil forces is

of the people, who "are the multitude bound together by the mutual recognition of rights and a mutual cooperation for the common good." The government should be for the good of the people. But what is for their good?

Augustine follows the Platonists in seeking out the ultimate good *Summum Bonum* toward which ethics aims (8, 8). "This is the good we seek for itself and not because of something else." And once we get it, we need nothing more to make us happy. It is a good which we enjoy (*frui*) in itself rather than using (*uti*) it for another purpose.

Extrinsic things such as honor, glory, power and wealth are relative goods which can be profitable for moral people but can be used badly by the wicked.

While other philosophers sought the ultimate good in the body, soul or whole person, the Platonists pursued it in a moral life. "Only those attain it who know and imitate God and find their blessedness wholly in this." The true philosopher, or lover of wisdom, is happy when he attains his highest good, God. "Ultimate good is not so much a good to end all goods, but rather one by which goodness reaches its fullest consummation" (19, 1).

Philosophers differ on the ends that people chose to aim their lives: bodily pleasure, calm, serenity, health, security, etc. But Augustine praises virtue. "The art of living derived from education. Of all the soul's goods it is the highest" (19, 3). Once virtue takes hold of our lives, she orients all other goods toward herself. Moreover, "there is absolutely no good, whether of soul or body, that virtue prefers to herself. For virtue makes good use of both herself and of all other goods which can make one happy." Without virtue goods are no longer goods, since there is no profit if they are used badly.

Social goods are most important in a society, "when the goods of one's friends are loved for what they are as we love our own possessions." And when we wish goods for our friends that we wish for ourselves. These friends can be one's own family, fellow citizens, the inhabited world or the whole cosmos of heaven and earth.

The social good and the sharing of it date back to the Golden Age of Saturn when all things were held in common. The Romans looked back with nostalgia to this ideal time of social good in later days when the patricians controlled most of the land for their own private profit.

The Stoics and later the Christians stressed sharing in the Saturnian ideal. Augustine, like many of the other Christian fathers and some emperors and philosophers, thought that there really should not be rich and poor people, for wealth should be a means to an end.[1]

Augustine contrasts the ideal of divine law in which temporal goods should be used to attain eternal good (*Free Choice* 1, 15) and human law which protects the right of ownership as long as peace and order are

---

also found in Zoroastrian, Intertestamental, New Testament, Early Christian and Manichaean literature.

1. See Mohler, *Late Have I Loved You* , 137-46.

preserved.[1] So for fear of losing their goods, they are deterred from harming others in their pursuit of business and the acquiring of wealth. Moreover, we should use (*uti*) our earthly goods to help us reach our final good, God, who alone is our ultimate joy (*frui*) (19, 14-16).

According to God's original plan one person should not be subject to another. But this happened because of sin. So without sin there would have been no slavery, servants, or superiors as in the Golden Age of Saturn.

Augustine gives an example of a wealthy and a middle class person in a large city. Who is happier? While the rich one is in constant fear of losing his possessions, the man of more modest means is content with less. Moreover, he is well loved by his family, pious and at peace with the world (4, 3).

Whereas the earth belongs to God by divine right, human law says, "This is mine." But the right to private property is limited by the Roman Code to sustain order in society. For those who use their wealth unjustly are really stealing other's property.

Is it not the Christian ideal to give up all in voluntary poverty to follow Christ? Obviously few Christians have heard this call. However, affluent Christians should be poor in spirit, not loving their gold and silver more than Christ, while giving of their surplus to the needy. Augustine lauds these successful Christians who are poor in Christ and are eminent in their charity (L 157). For many of the servants of God who criticize the wealthy Christians are, in turn, supported by them. The Church includes the rich and the voluntary and involuntary poor, leaders and followers, who mutually help each other.

Augustine encourages the sharing of our surplus with the needy (S 9), imitating Christ who was poor outside but rich with eternal life inside. Since pride is a disease of the affluent, they should humbly reach down to help the poor. Virtues, the riches of the heart, are more valuable than jewels and precious metals. Since God uses the wealthy to feed the poor, the moneyed are really sharing God's harvest, not their own.

Augustine, like the Bible, opposes usury for it takes advantage of the poor, in lieu of charity (S 86).

If pagans can share their abundance, a fortiori should the Christians (5, 16). For the Romans subordinated their private good for the common weal. Not only did they hold their personal avarice within bounds, but they kept themselves away from public crime, in order to receive honor, power and glory from their fellow citizens.

Roman law was highly respected worldwide, while their history and literature were greatly honored. So they received their reward here on earth

---

1. The Romans said that divine laws (*iura divina*) are created by the gods to regulate the relations of people to the gods, while human laws (*iura humana*) are created by people and protected by sanctions imposed by men. These laws govern the relations between people (B 527, 529), to minimize damage.

(see Mt 6:2-5). By contrast, the Christian martyrs who suffered at the hands of the Romans received their recompense in heaven.

We are here such a short time, does it matter what kind of government we live under (5, 17)? The Romans spread their law over the world by force. But later they made "the privilege of the few a fellowship of all," and they called all encompassed by the Empire citizens of Rome, except for the lower propertyless class, who lived off the public weal.

So what is the distinction between conquered and conquerors? True, the latter increase their pride by their victory. But otherwise they pay taxes, pursue education and are senators. Take away the boasting and all are alike.

They undergo such hardships as war for victory and honor in order to build up their earthly city. How much more should we do to gain our heavenly metropolis!

Augustine, a realistic pastor, discusses some of the problems of human societies beginning with the family (19, 5-11). "All history is a tale of slights and fights and spirits vexed." So misunderstandings and unpleasantries are common ailments in human society.

Battles begin in the home: husband and wife, parents and children, and, of course, in-laws (see Mt 10:36).[1] Often pretended friendships are based on personal and not social good.

But what about civil society? If problems are common in the bosom of the family, what can we expect in the city? Squabbles with neighbors, friends, acquaintances, colleagues, bosses, business competitors, robbers, etc. So we find a proliferation of civil suits, criminal indictments and a plethora of lawyers pursuing personal gain. And even worse, civil wars and seditions among rival gangs and factions. Moreover, the courts torture innocent victims to force them to confess to something they did not do.[2]

The third society is the world community. And the bigger the group, the more problems. Certainly the worldwide Roman Empire was falling apart at the time of Augustine due to the barbarian invasions and internal strife and corruption. One of the biggest obstacles to mutual understanding is the difference in languages between the Romans and their conquered satellites. So the victors tried to enforce uniformity of law and language throughout the Empire. But at what a price! "There is one war after another, havoc everywhere and tremendous slaughtering of men." There arose wars between the vanquished nations and Rome and within the countries themselves. We will discuss Augustine's philosophy of war and peace more in a later section.

Another conundrum faced in every human society on all levels is that we

---

1. Cicero, *In Verrem* 2, 1, 15.
2. *Quaestio per tormenta* in the Republic was reserved for slaves. However, in the Empire citizens could be tortured, though the *honestiores* only for severe crimes such as treason (*maiestas*), but *humiliores* also for lesser offenses. As the Roman Empire evolved, torture (*quaestio*) was used more frequently, though criticized by emperors and jurists because of the dubious value of forced confessions (D 48, 18, 1 pr.) (B 663, 738-39).

mistake our friends for enemies and vice-versa. For too often what appears to be true friendship is really pursued and cultivated for personal gain. And once the advantage is attained, the pseudo-fellowship is promptly dropped. We fear for our true friends lest they be struck by famine, war, illness, prison, slavery, etc. Or we may be anxious lest they prove unfaithful.

Also we are sad when our trusted friend is taken by death. For we cannot be indifferent to our true friends, our bonds of human fellowship and tender relationships. "It is impossible for us not to taste as bitter the death of those whose life for us was such a sense of sweetness." And our broken heart requires healing condolences. Yet physical bereavement is easier to take than a spiritual loss through serious sin or apostasy. On the other hand, when our friend dies a holy death we rejoice, although our heart may be broken. For he or she is now free from the painful sorrows of life (19, 8).

The Platonists (19, 9) saw also a fourth society (after the family, city and the world community)—a cosmic people, including heaven and earth, angels and devils. However, although our deceased friends are happy in heaven, we still mourn their passing. So cosmic society includes heaven where there are no more sorrow, hurts or temptations, but only "an eternally imperturbable peace." This is our final goal and good to which our whole earthly life points and hopes for.

Rome and the Church[1]

The Roman Empire was in many ways an extension of Rome with the Roman language, law and order. Rome, like Athens and most ancient cities, was united by a common ancestry, often from mythological progenitors. As the Greek cities were divided into philatries and associations, so Rome was separated into *familiae* and *gentes*.

Religion plays an important role in the founding and evolution of a city. With its household gods of the hearth and ancestors "each family constituted first and foremost a closed society which its own worship separated from other families" (15).

For larger social groups to develop there is a need of a unifying worship. These larger societies were associations (*gentes*), tribes or cities with common gods such as Zeus or Heracles. "The recognition of gods common to several families alone made possible the birth of the city" (15). Thus religious worship and social progress evolved together. This trend is seen in the history of most countries, where the sovereign hoped to unite his people under a new or old god. *Cuius regio, eius religio.*

Thus the Christian Roman emperors, beginning with Constantine, hoped

---

1. See E. Gilson, Foreword to Saint Augustine, *The City of God* (Garden City: Doubleday, 1953), 13-33.

that their new religion would be a unifying factor in the Empire. However, problems arose from without and within, as we have seen. So some of the pagans blamed the Church for the fall of Rome. First of all, Christian otherwordliness gave service to the Empire a low priority.

Also the Christian opposition to the popular Roman gods brought down the latter's retaliation on the Roman people. For example, the Christian martyrs were accused of the crime of *maiestas* in their preference of Christ over Augustus. As we mentioned earlier, Marcellinus wrote to Augustine concerning these early misunderstandings between Church and state. For example, how could the Christian doctrine of non-retaliation be compatible with the defense of Rome against her enemies? And how can we explain the deterioration of the Empire under the Christian emperors?

Augustine replies that before Christianity came to Rome, the pagans had practiced these same meek and mild virtues, as Sallust and Cicero have noted. Furthermore, Christian soldiers are not commanded to lay down their arms when they should be defending their country. Moreover, not only are Christians not forbidden to serve the state, but many of them as leaders, judges, senators, soldiers, families, slaves and farmers, build up Rome rather than weaken it (L 136).

Also, it is not the Christianity of the emperors that undermines Rome, but rather the decadence and luxury of a slave society, in which childbearing is replaced by promiscuity, while adultery, divorce and pleasure worsen marriage and the family, the foundation stones of Roman society.

Christianity has two purposes, according to Augustine. The first is to save human society, while the second is to build up a Christian society. Rome needs a reformation for it has fallen from its virtuous life of former times. But now divine authority comes through the Church, promoting morality, frugality, continence, friendship, justice and concord (L 138).

Good Christians make good citizens. Just as in ancient times Rome owed its success to the virtue of its people such as frugality, strength and purity. If these civil virtues bring prosperity, a fortiori, the moral practices of Christianity. "The sufficiency of the political virtues in their own order testifies to the supernatural specification of the Christian virtues both in their essence and end."

This is the old "a fortiori" argument which is the constant theme of early Christianity, namely, if pagans can be virtuous, a fortiori, the Christians should be so. Moreover, Christianity did not cause Roman decadence, since this moral weakness preceded the arrival of the Church in Rome.

However, this argument hardly swayed the pagans who blamed the fall of Rome on the Christian Alaric and his Gothic invasion of 410. So Augustine set to writing the history of the two cities of God and man in order to exonerate the Christians of these false accusations. Augustine's city of God is cosmic, including the whole universe here below and up in heaven.

Is Rome a city in the true sense of a place of justice and harmony? Hardly now, although it may have been so in ancient times. However, since even then Roman justice was imperfect, it was not a true society.

There is only one city that has perfect justice and that is the city of Christ. God intended the unity of man by his creation of Adam and Eve from whom all are descended. So all are natural brothers and sisters in Adam and Eve and can become spiritual brothers and sisters in Christ. And from the beginning there were two cities, good and evil, Abel and Cain.

The Romans claim that the long success of the Republic and the Empire was due to their gods, who rewarded their devotion (4, 3). However, it was not a happy time, since they lived in the midst of endless wars. As we have seen, wealthy people, cities or nations are unhappy for they are constantly in fear of losing what they have. Whereas those who have less are more at peace for they have less to lose.

> Fear of God and uprightness, God's great gifts, are enough for the true happiness of rulers, since this will enable them to spend this life well and thus win eternal life. (4, 3)

Moreover, their rule is a blessing on their subjects. On the other hand, wicked leaders, slaves of their vices, constantly test those living under them.

If the Roman gods prospered the growth of the Empire, how about the success of the Assyrians and the Persians? Who underwrote their expanding dominions? Certainly not the Roman deities (4, 5-8).

What about Jupiter, the head of all the gods? If he is the one true god why do they make graven images of him and provide a wife Juno? And so of Neptune and Pluto, each in charge of part of the world, plus many lesser gods in a confusing mixture. Many superstitious beliefs of the Romans were criticized by Cicero and Varro. By contrast the one true Christian God is a preferred remedy (4, 29-34).

Since the Roman gods are not responsible for the success of the Empire, why did the true God allow it to expand (5, 1)? "Divine providence alone explains the establishment of kingdoms among the people."

Two Loves, Two Cities[1]

As Gilson reminds us,[2] Augustine's two cities are really mystical metropolises. First, the city of those who love God in Christ and who will enjoy eternal life with him in heaven. And second, the city of those who do not love God

---

1. For the Romans all citizens (*cives*) of a political unit (state, city, colony or municipality) form a *civitas*. It can also refer to an autonomous unit such as the Roman state or a foreign state (B 389).

2. Gilson, *Christian Philosophy,* 26-35.

and who will suffer eternal damnation in hell. Love of God and love of the world constitute the two cities.

In his *Literal Commentary on Genesis* (A) (11, 15) Augustine describes the two loves as an exaggerated self deification and Christian charity. Perhaps this distinction is compatible with the classes we saw earlier, namely, our own private good and shared social good; one profane and the other holy.

One love is social, while the other is selfish. One seeks out the common good with a view to eternal life, while the other channels the common wealth for its own profit because of the need to be over others. While the love of God is subject to him, the love of man approaches self-glorification. And as the first love is serene and quiet the second is angry and querulous. Moreover, the former is truthful and friendly, whereas the latter needs false flattery and is jealous. And whereas the first seeks the neighbor's good, the second wants to dominate him or her.

The two cities were found among the angels before humans were created and formed their own municipalities, the good uniting with the angels and their king for eternal life, while the bad join the fallen angels and Satan to be cast into exterior darkness. "Tell me what a people loves and I will tell you who the people are."

The two cities are personified by Jerusalem, a vision of peace, and Babylon, or confusion. The cities include believers and unbelievers, religious and irreligious, lovers of God and lovers of self, the city of God and the city of the devil.

> It was enough that the city of God exist in order to inspire people with the desire to organize the earth into a single society made to the image and likeness of the heavenly city. (32)

Augustine's two cities are mystical and supernatural. The former is a city of good order, peace, a true society of the spirit, whereas the latter is a city of error, evil, disorder and confusion of flesh, hardly worthy of the name of society.

Commenting on Psalm 65 (N), Augustine notes that when the captive Israelites were led into Babylon, Jeremiah promised them freedom in seventy years in order to rebuild Jerusalem. And so it happened. Paul saw this as a figure of the persecutions of his day.

So also "we ought to know first our activity, then our deliverance. We ought to know the Babylon wherein we are captives and the Jerusalem for a return to which we are sighing."

"Therefore, that city [Jerusalem], being one earthly, did bear the figure of a certain city everlasting in the heavens." However, the second city superseded the first, whose temple was destroyed. Yet we are still in captivity as long as we live in our bodies (see 2 Cor 5:6).

The two cities, Babylon and Jerusalem, confusion and peace. "Observe now the city of confusion in order that you may perceive the vision of peace. To endure that city, sigh for this one."

The two cities are mingled here below. While Jerusalem was founded by Abel, Babylon was planned by Cain. Moreover, the two urban centers are motivated by two loves. "Whereas the love of God makes Jerusalem, the love of the world builds up Babylon." Ask yourself what you love and you will find out what city you belong to. If you find out that you live in Babylon, replace your lust with charity. And if you inhabit Jerusalem, endure your captivity while hoping for freedom.

"Now, therefore, let us hear of, brothers and sisters, hear of, and sing of, and long for that city whereof we are citizens," so that we may form a love of that city which we had forgotten. However, the captives in Babylon turned away from God and toward their enemies.

Nevertheless, an inexplicable sight is promised. "And this is God himself who has built the city."

> Already longing, we are there, already in hope into that land. We set
> it before us like an anchor lest, being tossed by the angry sea, we
> suffer shipwreck.

Though we are tempted on our journey, our hope is still grounded in Jerusalem. Moreover, while we long for Jerusalem our corruptible flesh cannot harm us. "Peace shall conquer and war shall be ended." And the conquering city is a vision of peace.

Psalm 99. Sion-Jerusalem is the city of God. Sion signifies sight and contemplation to watch and look forward to. "Every soul is a Sion, if it tries to see the light of God."

Sion is the city of God and the Church.

> For those who love one another and who love their God who dwells
> in them, constitute a city unto God. Because a city is held together
> by some law, their law is love, and that very love is God.

Since God is love, if we are full of love, we are full of God. "And many full of love constitute a city full of God."

In his *The City of God*, book 14, Augustine further discusses the two loves that inspire the two cities. Though God intended unity in the human race, descended from one ancestor, his plan was spoiled by disobedience. So the human race was divided into those who live according to the flesh and those who live according to the spirit, each pursuing peace in their own way.

By flesh scripture means the whole human nature including body and soul. Paul lists many sins as works of the flesh. For example, immorality, murder, drunkenness, parties, but also vices of the soul such as contention, anger, envy and pride (see Gal 5:19-21).

But we cannot blame our sins on the flesh, for God made our flesh good. However, it is not right to abandon God for created goods. Our good will is a work of God, while our bad will is a human work and a turning away from God (14, 11).

Pride led Adam and Eve to sin and so it is the main vice in the city of man and is personified in the devil. On the other hand, humility is the vexilla of the city of God (14, 13). This is especially seen in Christ our head.

> The humble city is the society of holy men and good angels, whereas the proud city is the society of wicked people and evil angels. The one city began with the love of God; the other had its beginnings in the love of self.

"Whoever seeks to become more than he or she is becomes less." And while we aspire to be self-sufficient, we retire from him who is truly sufficient for us.

> Two societies have issued from two kinds of love. A worldly association has flowered from a selfish love which dared to despise even God, whereas the communion of saints is rooted in a love of God that is ready to trample on self.

While the latter relies on the Lord, the other is independent. Whereas the city of man wants only insincere flattery, the city of God wants only to hear God.

In the worldly city rulers and people want to dominate others. "But in the city of God all the citizens serve one another in charity." And while in the city of man leaders are admired for their strength, the city of God finds its vigor and grace in the Lord. Whereas in the human city they pursue personal gain, in the city of God there is love, piety and worship of the supreme One. In books 15-18 Augustine traces the evolution of the two cities through history.

Justice and Law

Roman politics is built on justice, since justice is necessary for the harmony and peace of the city.[1] Augustine feels that because Rome had lost its sense of justice, it is no longer a city. Yet Roman law and justice would become the foundation of European jurisprudence in both Church and state.

Scipio noted that not only can a state be governed without injustice, but it must be ruled with an absolute justice (*Republic* 2, 42). "You have a true

---

1. Gilson, *Christian Philosophy*, 22-23. Justice (*iustitia*) is "the constant and perpetual desire to render every one his due" (*Institutes* 1, 1; D 1, 1) (B 535). *Ius* (law or right) is "the art of finding the good and the equitable" (Celcius) (D 1, 1, 1 pr.). Also "What is just and fair (*aequum et bonum*) is called *ius*" (Paul) (D 1, 1, 11 pr.) (B 525). The fundamental principles (*praecepta*) of *ius* are: 1. To live honestly, 2. Not to do harm to anybody, and 3. To give everyone what is his (B 525).

commonwealth, that is, the weal of the people, when it is rightly and justly administered either by one monarch, by a few men or by all the people." But what if the king, aristocrats or the people themselves are unjust? Then not only is the commonwealth bad, but it is not a commonwealth at all.

A tyrant or a faction does not pursue the control of a country for the welfare of the people, but for their own self-interest. Moreover, an unjust people would lose their self-identity as a "multitude bound together by a common recognition of rights, and a mutual cooperation for the common good." Thus the corrupt Roman republic described by Sallust and Cicero was no republic at all.

Augustine believes that Rome was never a true republic, even in olden times. "True justice is not found save in that commonwealth, if we may so call it, whose founder and ruler is Jesus Christ," for the weal of the people and for true justice.

What is injustice, but organized brigandage and petty kingdoms (4, 4)? "Groups of men, under the rule of a leader, bound together by a common agreement, dividing their booty according to a settled principle." When they conquer cities and countries, they are called a kingdom, not because of the common good but because of their impunity.

On the other hand, the happy Christian ruler governs with justice (5, 24), and is not puffed up by flattery. Thus his sovereignty is a divine ministry of true religion. He fears, loves and worships God, while cherishing the kingdom which he shares with all Christians. Slow to punish and quick to forgive, he disciplines only when he is forced to do so by order and security. Moreover, he pardons with a hope of reform, tempered by mercy and generosity. He is more interested in curbing his own lusts than in ruling the whole world. The true Christian emperor is happy now in hope of his future joy of eternal life.

What is justice? Externally it guarantees that each is given what belongs to each. Interiorly it ensures that our soul is subject to God and our body is under the guidance of our soul, while our body and soul together are obedient to the Lord. Meanwhile our struggle goes on against our fleshy lusts and we continue to forget God, as our moral diseases weaken our virtue of justice (19, 4).

As we have seen, Scipio demands true justice as a solid foundation of the republic (19, 21). "What is rightly done is justly done." Thus bad human laws are wrong, "since even unjust lawgivers call a right (*ius*) only what derives from the fountainhead of justice (*iustitia*)." This opposes those who claim that a right (*ius*) is whatever is useful (*utile*) to the one in power.

So wherever true justice is lacking, there cannot be a people who mutually recognize each others' rights (*iures*). Rather we have an unruly mob with no interest in the common good nor with any human respect for each other. Furthermore, where there are no rights or justice, there is no commonwealth.

"Justice is the virtue which accords to each what is his or her due." But what of those who deny God his rights over us and give themselves to demons?

The two cities of God and man are built on two loves regulated by two laws, human and divine. On the one hand, the city of man loves creatures such as honor, glory, power, wealth and pleasure. So human law tries to minimize the damage done to society by the unbridled pursuit of these ephemeral goals. On the other hand, the city of God loves God and divine law safeguards this direction (*On Free Choice* 1, 15).

Roman law could confiscate goods that were used in a way harmful to society. "The law does not punish the sin committed by loving these things, but rather the crime of taking them from others unjustly."[1]

In this vein Augustine writes to Macedonius, Vicar of Africa (L 153) (414).

> He who uses his wealth badly, possesses it wrongfully; and wrongful possession means that it is another's property. . . . Money is wrongly possessed by bad people, while the good ones who love it least have the best right to it.
>
> In this life the wrong of evil possessors is endured and among them certain laws are established which are called civil laws, not because they force people to make good use of their riches, but because those who make bad use of them become thereby less injurious.

Augustine recommends mercy toward evil-doers. For "if evil-doers did not find Him merciful, there would be no good people." Augustine himself gave good example of kindness to the erring, though Macedonius thought he was interfering in the judicial system (L 42).

But do we have any claim at all to our private property? And, if so, is it by divine or human right (*On John* 6, 25-26)? It is by the human laws of kings, since "the earth is the Lord's and the fullness thereof" (Ps 24, 1). And God's good earth supports the poor and rich alike. The human right which says "this is mine" God has given to us through emperors and kings.

Augustine notes (5, 15) that the pagan Romans subordinated their private property for the common good, while keeping their public and personal ambitions in check. However, they have been rewarded by worldly acclaim. If the Romans are honored for observing human law, a fortiori, the citizens of the city of God who inherit eternal life.

---

1. The concept of ownership (*dominium*) appears at the end of the Republic. However, it can be limited if it violates public order or it does not promote the best interests of the community (*utilitas publica*). Private property can even be expropriated through compulsory purchase (D 41, 1) (B 441).

Peace and War[1]

The history of the city of man is the history of war, whereas the city of God is a city of peace. But how about the famous Pax Romana?[2] It was only achieved by forcing law, language and worship on its empire. "But at what a cost! There is one war after another," turmoil and senseless killing everywhere (19, 7).

However, Augustine adds (4, 15) (F) that the Empire expanded because of just wars against wicked enemies.[3] Otherwise Rome would have remained a small country, which, along with other nations would constitute one big family.

"Wars and conquests may rejoice unprincipled people, but are a sad necessity in the eyes of those who live by principle." However, it would be worse if evil-doers dominated the just. But even this condition can be seen as fortunate in the light of eternity. Nevertheless, it is better to have a friendly neighbor "than to have to subdue one who has taken up arms against you." Moreover, we should never hope for an obstreperous neighbor just so we will have someone to beat up on. Wicked peoples had much to do with the expansion of the empire through the defeat of their nations. So why not make Wickedness and Victory goddesses?

Though the general aim is for peace, yet wars seem to generate only new battles. Augustine realistically notes that there never has been, nor is today, "any absence of hostile foreign powers to provoke war." Moreover, as the empire expands, civil strife and social tensions increase within. Frequent and cruel massacres are just one part of the ravages of war (19, 7).

But good rulers only wage just wars. "A good man would be under compulsion to wage no wars at all, if there were no such things as just wars." A war is only justified by the attack of an unjust aggressor. "And that injustice ought to be a source of grief to any good person."

As the vagaries of the world continue to assail us, we long more and more for heavenly peace, "which is unshakable and unending." They all will be healed by wisdom and the resurrection of the body, no longer fighting our rowdy passions, but rather enjoying "an imperturbable peace" (19, 10), consummate beatitude and limitless perfection.

---

1. This section first appeared in *The Priest*, February, 1992.
2. *Pia et aeterna pax* (just and everlasting peace) is arranged through a solemn treaty (*foedus*), including: peace (*pax*), friendship (*amicitia*) and common political interests (*societas*). Special embassies and the consent of the people and the senate are involved, while in the Empire, the emperor concluded peace (Gaius, *Institutes* 3, 94) (B 623).
3. Roman tradition says that Romulus gave his people the right to declare war (*bellum indicere*). Cicero adds (*Republic* 2, 17, 31) that the third king of Rome, Tullus Hostilius, gave the priests (*fetiales*) the power to declare war formally. Moreover, without this act the war was declared unjust and evil (*injustum et impium*). During the Republic the *comitia centuriata* (military voting groups of one hundred persons) had the power to declare war (*lex de bello indicendo*) (B 372, 398).

Though we can enjoy partial peace here on earth, it seems like misery in comparison to eternal life. When we live in peace with our neighbors, this is really a part of virtue and the right use of this world's goods, though at best a temporal peace. And even if we do not bask in an earthly peace, then virtue helps us use our sufferings along with our blessings toward "a peace so good that no peace could be better, a peace so great that a greater one would be impossible." Peace is our highest good (see Ps 146). "He has placed peace in your borders" (19, 11), that peace which is our final good—Jerusalem, the vision of peace.

Even on the earthly level there is nothing more desirable and welcome as peace. "Even when waging war, every man wants peace, whereas no one desires war while he is making peace" (19, 12). For truly seditions, secessions and brigandage aim at peace. Peace is especially the goal in the household with all living in harmony under the *pater familias*.

All want peace in their own way and in their own society. "When they go to war, what they want is to make, if they can, their enemies their own and then to impose on them the victor's will and then call it peace."

Even the bad and solitary Kakos of Greek mythology wanted peace "in which no force would do him harm or disturb his rest." Beginning with a peaceful body, what looked like injustice, greed and savagery was really self-preservation.

Even animals want peace. And much more so human beings. "Even when wicked men go to war, they want peace for their own society and the only way to ensure peaceful submission is by force." Sinful man wants to replace the equality of all under God by his own domination. "He hates the peace of God which is just, preferring his own unjust peace." However, his unjust tranquility is not worthy of the name.

Even a dead body finds peace in the graveyard where its dissolution serves the common good of nature. And the peace of a living body is the ordered equilibrium of all its parts. While the peace of beasts is a balancing of their appetites, human peace is the harmonious correspondence of conduct and conviction (19, 13). Moreover, the peace of the body and soul working together is well-ordered life and health.

Many wars are due to frustrated human desires (18, 2) (F). Though in the ideal order a community should be one big happy family, "each individual is driven by his or her passions to pursue private goods." However, there is not enough to go around. Why not? Simply "because only Absolute Being can satisfy human nature."

Why do we need the state anyway? Because in the city of man people's greed and desires get the better of them without some sort of government to keep a modicum of peace. So the state serves a utilitarian purpose so that its citizens can enjoy their desires without harming each other in the process.

Yet there remains a continual tension in the community, like a chronic condition of civil war. Under constant pressure from the successful, "they prefer sheer survival and any kind of peaceful settlement to their own continued hegemony, even to liberty itself." Better to bow down before the conqueror, "than to risk wholesale annihilation" (18, 2). God who has charge of victory and defeat, gives supremacy to some and subjugation to others.

Peace between human beings and God is an ordered obedience guided by faith and under divine law, while peace between humans is a well regulated fellowship. Beginning in the home, "it is the ordered harmony of authority and obedience between the members of a family living together." And political peace is "the ordered harmony of authority and obedience between citizens."

The peace of the city of God "is a perfectly ordered and harmonious communion of those who find their joy in God and in one another in God."

Finally, peace "is the calm that comes of order." But what is order? "An arrangement of like and unlike things whereby each of them is disposed in its proper place." Unhappy people are not at peace, "since they lack the calm of that Order which is beyond every storm." Though they do not share the tranquility of the blessed, this very separation is the result of the law of order.

Even miserable people can temporarily adjust to their pain and so attain a measure of peace. However, they are not free from worry and suffering. But their peace has to be in harmony with natural law. Although they are in pain, they may retain some measure of peace if their agony is not too acute and their body does not disintegrate in the process. Moreover, there can be no pain without life. In fact, our pangs signal us that our life is threatened.

Likewise "there is no war that does not suppose some kind of peace. . . . War, insofar as those who wage it or have it waged upon them are beings with organic natures, involves peace." To be organic means to be ordered, and so at peace (19, 13).

"Anyone who grieves over the loss of peace to his nature does so out of some remnant of that peace wherewith his nature loves itself." God, creator and ordainer, has given us a temporal peace to help us survive here below. For example, health, security, friendship and other gifts to help us preserve or regain peace: sunshine, clean air and water and all the aid we get to feed, clothe and beautify our bodies.

If we use these gifts of our mortal peace properly, we will receive eternal peace and the eternal enjoyment of God and our neighbors in heaven.

> In the earthly city temporal goods are to be used with a view to the enjoyment of earthly peace, whereas in the heavenly city they are used with a view to the enjoyment of eternal peace.

This is the old *uti/frui* theme again, namely, creatures are to be used to help us attain eternal life and not to be enjoyed only for our own personal pleasure. God alone is our ultimate joy!

If we were animals we would pursue the order between our appetites and their objects, so that our bodily peace might aid our peace of soul.

For if order in the body is lacking, the peace of an irrational soul is checked, since it cannot attain the satisfaction of its appetites.

Both these forms of peace subserve the mutual peace of body and soul, "the peace of life and health in good order."

Human beings make all the peace and order we share with animals serve the peace of our rational soul. But we cannot do this without divine guidance. Thus all the peace of our body and soul is ordered "to that higher peace which unites us to God—an ordered obedience, directed by faith and under God's eternal law of love."

This is the twofold love of God and neighbor and the mutual help of neighbors. "Out of this love we will arrive at peace—as much as in us lies—at that peace which is a regulated fellowship," starting in our own home with "the harmonious interplay of authority and obedience among those who live there," husband and wife, parents and children, master and servants.

In the Christian home of the city of God, "those who command serve those whom they appear to rule—because, of course, they do not command out of lust to domineer, but out of a sense of duty," not out of pride, but from solicitude.

It was not God's original plan to have some people over others, but rather he gave them dominion over animals (19, 15). Thus in ancient times holy men became shepherds rather than kings. Because God wished in this way to teach us that the normal hierarchy of creatures is different from that which sin has made imperative. This attitude is reflected in Augustine's episcopate where he works alongside of his people with concern for their welfare, rather than over or ahead of them (*prodesse non praeesse*).

Slaves *servi* are an important product of wars in which healthy young captives are saved from death *servabantur*. Augustine sees slavery also as a result of sin so that one person is subject to another.

Paul advises slaves to serve their masters "until injustice becomes a thing of the past and every human sovereignty and power is done away with, so that God may be all in all."

The Roman *pater familias* had equal concern for his slaves and children. Moreover, anyone who violates domestic harmony is to be punished (19, 16). And since the home is the foundation stone of civil society, "it follows that domestic peace has a relation to political peace." Thus authority and obedience in the family are related to authority and obedience in the city.

This explains why a father must apply certain regulations of civil law to the governance of his home so as to make it accord with the peace of the whole community.[1]

---

1. The Roman *pater familias* had to be a citizen and not under the power of another (*patria potestas*). He is the head of the family (*princeps*) and has dominion over them.

The home of unbelievers pursues a temporal peace by the acquiring of earthly possessions, while the home of the faithful is concerned with enjoying heavenly peace in which nothing can interfere (19, 17).

> The faithless earthly metropolis seeks only a terrestrial peace, and limits the goal of its peace, of its harmony of authority and obedience among its citizens, to the voluntary and collective attainment of objectives necessary to mortal existence.

The heavenly city, on the other hand, while on its earthly pilgrimage lives by faith and so "must use this earthly peace until such time as our mortality, which needs such peace, passes away." So as long as the city of God exists here below, "she has no hesitation about keeping in step with the civil law which governs matters pertaining to our existence on earth." Since our mortal life is the same for all, there should be a common cause between the two cities in our every day living.

While the city of God is a wayfarer she welcomes all nations of diverse languages, customs, etc. And so she maintains a human peace with great toleration provided that their practices do not go against the belief and worship of the one, true God. The city of God subordinates earthly peace to the heavenly harmony. For the only real peace is "the perfectly ordered and harmonious communion of those who find their joy in God and in one another in God." In this peace we are no longer anxious about our health or life. Rather we are perfectly happy in our spiritual body which is under the complete control of our will. This peace our pilgrim city enjoys here in faith until its heavenly completion, referring its good deeds in this direction.

The supreme good of the city of God "is everlasting and perfect peace and not merely a continuing peace which individually mortal men enter upon and leave by birth and death." But rather they live in immortality without any adversity—a happy life, which we can anticipate here in hope—the everlasting and flawless peace of heaven (19, 20).

So the city of God has peace with God, here in faith, while in heaven by vision. However, here below our peace is at best temporary (19, 27), for we are still battling the forces of evil (see Job 7:1).

> In that final peace which is the end and purpose of all virtue here on earth, our nature, made whole by immortality and incorruption, will have no vices and experience no rebellion from within or without.

God will govern us and our soul will be over our body. "And the happiness in eternal life and law will make obedience sweet and easy in everlasting life." "This peace of such blessedness or the blessedness of such peace is to be our supreme good." Moreover, if eternal peace is the reward of the just, then eternal war must be the punishment of the unjust, with the will and passion battling each other without any hope of victory.

Happiness here below is at best ephemeral. For example, the famous Pax

Romana. How can there be hope or peace "in people perpetually living amid the horrors of war, perpetually wading in blood," constantly haunted by fear and driven by murderous passions. For there can be no solid happiness without fear here below. For example, the wealthy live in fear of losing their riches.

If people are ruled in justice, there can be a measure of happiness and peace in a kingdom (4, 3-4). Injustice, on the other hand, makes sovereignty organized brigandage. Thus the Romans imposed their laws on conquered countries by war and slaughter. Though they could have succeeded just as well by diplomacy, there would have been less glory in victory.

Moreover, the Roman conquests could have been won without the aid of Mars, Belona and Victoria. "But no war, no victory; and that would have put the Romans on the same level with other people." Later they would make all the inhabitants of the Empire—except for the lower class—citizens of Rome (5, 17).

Augustine the realist sees the city of man as a "city of contention with opinions divided by foreign wars and domestic quarrels and by the demands for victories which either end in death or are merely momentary respites from further war" (15, 4).

Whatever part of the global city goes to war, its aim is to conquer the world and it is hypnotized by its own evil. And even when such a city conquers, it is overcome by pride. However, if it is afraid of future challenges, "then the victory is only momentary." For "the power to reach domination by war is not the same as the power to remain in perpetual control."

Yet in all this the aim is for peace. "The purpose even of war is peace. For where victory is not followed by resistance, there is peace." This remains true as long as the two nations are not still jousting for some material good that is insufficient to share. "This kind of peace is a product of the work of war. And its price is a so-called glorious victory." Moreover, when the victory goes to the people with the juster cause, there is rejoicing in peace. Of course, the ultimate victory of the city of God will bring eternal peace.

Wars and strife have been the history of the city of man from the beginning, for example, Romulus and Remus, Cain and Abel—either for dominion or for envy. While the former is seen in the city of man, the latter battle is fought between the two cities. "Thus we have two wars, that of the wicked at war with the wicked, and that of the wicked at war with the good.

This was not the way it was in the beginning when kings were more concerned with protecting their borders than extending them. Ninus, the Assyrian, was the first to make war on neighboring nations, escalating his conquests more and more (4, 6). "Can waging war on neighbors and then by a series of wars crushing and enslaving peaceful peoples be called anything but colossal brigandage?"

Augustine, quoting Cicero (*Republic*, book 3), notes that "no good society should ever go to war unless it be in the defense of fidelity or of safety." Though it is natural for individuals to pass away, for a state to die is unacceptable. Thus a society must defend its permanence as a political community, like an evergreen tree which, though it loses some leaves, remains verdant. Of course, true safety is found only in the city of God (22, 6).

Who should make the decision for or against war? Augustine answers Faustus (22, 75-76) (N).

> The natural order which seeks the peace of mankind ordains that the monarch should have the power of undertaking war if he thinks it advisable.

So his soldiers should fight for the peace and safety of the state. When God orders a war to rebuke a nation, it is a righteous war.

But what if an evil king declares war? God either orders or permits it. Soldiers under a bad monarch should go into battle. Why? Because in some cases it is God's will and in other cases the military should obey their duty to wage war.

If God commands us to go to war, how much more so should we obey him rather than a human leader. But did not Jesus instruct us to turn the other cheek? (see Mt 5:20). Here Jesus wants an inner spirit rather than bodily actions. Do not fear those who can kill the body but not the soul (see Mt 10:16, 28, 30).

How do we know if our actions will have good or bad results (78)? "In time of peace, to reign or to serve, or to be at ease or to die. Or in time of war, to command or to fight, or to conquer or to be killed." Whatever is good is a divine blessing, while what is bad is a divine judgment.

But was not Christ a pacifist? How does this justify a Christian going to war? Augustine writes to Marcellinus (L 138) (412) (F) to show him that Christ's meekness and forgiveness are not incompatible with discipline and the punishing of evil in a Christian city. For surely war can be used as an instrument of God's justice in fighting evil.

Mutual agreement constitutes the state and also the Church. For example, Christ tells us to turn the other cheek, give away our cloak, etc. (see Mt 5:39-41). Thus we overcome evil by doing good with the hope of converting the evil one. This is the theme found in many of the martyrs. For interior patience is more important than external actions.

However, "we often have to act with a sort of kindly harshness when we are trying to make unwilling souls yield because we have to consider their welfare rather than their inclination." As a father punishes his son, curing him with an unwilling suffering.

> If the earthly state observes these Christian teachings, even war will not be waged without kindness. And it will be easier for a society whose peace is based on piety and justice to take thought for the conquered.

Thus one who is kept from evil suffers a useful restraint.

A sign of mercy—"that even wars should be waged by the good, in order to curb licentious passions by destroying those vices which should have been rooted out and suppressed by the rightful government."

But does not the Christian Church condemn war? Christ advises soldiers against violence, calumny and contentions over pay (see Lk 3:14). However, he does not tell them to quit the army. Moreover, many Christians faithfully served Rome as soldiers and officials.

Augustine writes to Marcellinus again (L 139) (412), advising officials against the use of capital punishment against the Donatists. Rather they should try to convert the heretics. However, Augustine believes that the secular arm can be helpful in putting down religious factions in order to promote the public weal.

Augustine also writes to the tribune Boniface on the correction of the Donatists (L 185) (417) (F). Though force may be used, capital punishment should be avoided.

Again he pens to Boniface, now Roman vicar of Africa (L 189) (418), who feels torn between the two cities. For he believes that serving God is incompatible with soldiering. So Augustine gives him some examples of good soldiers who also served God well. For example, King David and his men in the Old Testament and the Centurion (see Mt 8:8-10), Cornelius (Acts 10:1-8) and those who sought the advice of John the Baptizer (see Lk 3:12-14) in the New Testament. Moreover, while some holy Christian monks fight against the devil through their prayers and fasting, "you strive for them against visible barbarians by fighting."

When you arm for battle, think of your strength and skills as gifts of God. And they will be used as God wishes. Keep your pledged word with enemies and allies alike.

Hold onto peace, while waging war only out of necessity. "Peace is not sought for the purpose of stirring up war. But war is waged for the purpose of securing peace." Count Boniface should be a peacemaker even in battle in order to show the enemy the desirability of peace (see Mt 5:9). Furthermore, if human peace is so great, how much more valuable is the eternal, divine repose.

> Just as violence is meted out to him who rebels and resists, so mercy is due to him who is defeated and captured, especially where no disturbance of peace is to be feared.

In the latter part of the letter Augustine gives Boniface advice on how to lead a virtuous life, for our pilgrimage on earth is one long battle against the temptations of the city of man.

Augustine writes to Darius, a court official, to try to make peace between Count Boniface and the Vandals (L 229) (F) (429). "Blessed are the peacemakers." Which is better, war or peace? Though some vanquish their enemies with God's help, and so bring peace, "it is a greater glory to destroy war with a word than to kill men with a sword and to secure and maintain peace rather than by war. It is true that good men often seek peace through war." But while others may kill, "on you rests the blessedness of forestalling the taking of life."

Conclusion

People gather together by mutual accord into societies: family, city, empire and globe, with human laws regulating their interests and interrelationships so that a measure of peace is attained.

Some of the pagan Romans accused the Christians of ruining the Empire by the Christian barbarian invasions, their stress on the heavenly kingdom to the neglect of the service to the Empire and their angering of the pagan gods.

Augustine responds in his book about the two cities of man and God. Both societies go along together until the final separation on judgment day.

The city of man is founded on natural love, law, justice and peace, which is at best an accommodation of sinful human nature in its pursuit of honor, glory, wealth and power. Mutual respect of rights is essential for even a temporal peace.

However, the final perfect goal of the Christian is eternal love and peace and perfect justice under the divine law of the city of God. Human justice, peace and law are just means to our eternal goal of the heavenly kingdom.

The two cities are mixed while we are on our earthly pilgrimage. And, indeed, both cities battle within our souls and bodies until we reach our final destination.

Psalm 136, "By the waters of Babylon we sat down and wept when we remembered Sion."

> There are two cities, for the present outwardly mingled together, yet separated in heart, running together through the course of time until the end; one whose end is everlasting peace and it is called Jerusalem. The other whose joy is peace in this world and it is called Babylon.

While living in Babylon "sigh for the everlasting Jerusalem. Whither your hope goes before, let your life follow. For there we shall be with Christ."

EPILOGUE

The Trinity

Augustine starts out his discussion of the Trinity with the one divine nature which the three persons share as they also partake of the common operations of the Godhead, although the incarnation and sanctification are appropriated to the Son and the Holy Spirit. The latter is the gift of love proceeding from the Father and the Son as from a single principle.

Augustine shows his people many natural and human triads, reflecting their triune Creator. However, we most resemble God, when we remember, understand and love him.

Augustine did much to harmonize the divinity of the Son and the Holy Spirit with the unity of God, opposing both tritheism and modalism.

Augustine has been called the first Christian psychologist for his study of the human soul and its faculties: memory, intellect and will, mirroring the Trinity.

Jesus Christ

Like his mentor Paul, Augustine was converted to Christ, his savior and mediator, priest and sacrifice, Son of God, Son of Man, power and wisdom. Though the only begotten Son of God, he is the brother of the Father's adopted sons and daughters. And although he is God, he was born a slave. The Word of God to men and women, God of God, light of light, fulfiller of the prophecies, atoner for sin, truth, consubstantial and coeternal with the Father.

Ruler of the world, he is present in a tiny baby. He is one person, both God and man, founder of the city of God. Word become flesh, born of a virgin, Son of Man. Divinely generated for human regeneration. Eternally born of the Father without a mother, yet born in time of a mother without a father. The Word of God became a speechless infant. God became human so that humankind could become God.

159

Although this is an unspeakable mystery, Augustine is driven to talk about it to his flock. For in our baptism we die and rise with Christ, who has atoned for our sins because he is both spirit and flesh, God and man, body and soul.

Blessed Virgin Mary

Mother Mary was honored as the paradigm of the virgin mother Church. Augustine's mariology, influenced by Ambrose and Jerome, taught that the Blessed Mother was virgin before, during and after the birth of her Son. Moreover, her virginity is a model for both the virgin Church and the virgins of the Church. Mary's faith is a prerequisite for her motherhood of Christ for she is mother of the Savior because she does the will of the Father. And so she is also mother of the body of Christ.

Augustine's Christmas sermons epitomize his mariology for on this day she brought forth her Son. The Church, parent of Christ in mind, but not in body, is both mother and virgin, giving birth to her children in baptism. While Mary has one Son, the Church has many sons and daughters gathered into one mystical body of Christ. The woman whom Christ created became his mother. A sublime mystery!

The Church

Augustine saw many prototypes of the Church in the Bible. For example, paradise, Eve, Noah's ark, Solomon's temple, etc. Moreover, as Israel is the spouse of Yahweh, so the Church, the new Israel, is the bride of Christ, as Paul teaches. Like Mary, who is both mother and virgin.

The Church is also the mystical body, or corporate personality of Christ. This is a mutual indwelling, for Christ is the head of the Church, while we are her members. Also the Church is both one and divers, as on Pentecost were seen and heard one dove and many tongues.

Augustine objects to those who want a perfect Church without any sinners. For Christ came to save the errant. The Church unifies her many members and is holy despite the presence of imperfect Christians in her body. The Church is also apostolic with her succession of bishops going back to the apostles. Moreover, since she is universally found throughout the Roman Empire, heretics should agree with the common consensus of the bishops. Some see Christ's Church as the visible city of God or kingdom of God, inspiring the city of man.

Authority

Authority is basically a builder, a supplier of a need. Thus Augustine uses the authority of Christ, his Church and scripture to build up his faith in the sacred mysteries. He relies on the firm faith of the universal Church as illustrated by his sainted mother and other Christian models such as Victorinus and Ambrose.

This divine authority helps heal Augustine's wounded soul and intellect. Moreover, it is freely given. Thus God through his only Son and his Church and scripture is the divine tutor of his pupil Augustine, building him up in his weakness, while, at the same time saving him from the many false claimants of divine authority.

The Clergy

Though the Judaeo-Christian tradition taught the priesthood of the laity, both cultures developed a ministry of priests, rabbis, presbyters, bishops, deacons, etc. The Christian clergy reflect a syncretism of Jewish and Roman customs. While the priest or bishop is the external agent of the sacraments, it is Christ himself who interiorly confects them.

Augustine followed Paul's requirements for the clergy, although the African bishop stressed celibacy vis-a-vis Paul's man of one wife. The two main ministerial jobs are: preaching the word of God and presiding at the mysteries.

Augustine talks much of his ministry in Hippo, to which he was chosen by the people. He wants to imitate the good shepherd rather than the selfish hireling. Moreover, he is not so much over his flock, but rather a fellow sheep along with them.

What should be done with bad priests? The apostles were far from perfect, so also is Augustine. However, public sinners should be kept from the ministry. In the last analysis, do what they say, not what they do.

The Sacraments

Augustine teaches the incarnational Christ, Church and sacraments. All include the visible and the invisible. Moreover, some sacraments such as baptism and order give their recipient indelible marks so they cannot be repeated.

There are many types of the sacraments, for example, the ark and flood prefigure baptism, while Melchizedek's meal and the manna of the desert anticipate the eucharist.

Augustine opposed the Donatists who insisted on the worthiness of the ministers, for Christ is the invisible priest who celebrates the mysteries. Augustine favored infant baptism as a remedy for original sin and the doorway to the incorporation in the body of Christ, the eucharist and eternal life. Though baptism outside of the Church is valid, it is not wholly effective until one is welcomed into the Church.

The eucharist commemorates the Passover meal of Jesus and his *haburah*. While the visible sacrament includes the bread and wine, we receive the invisible body and blood of Christ. The eucharist is the sign of Church unity—one bread, one body. By eating the body of Christ we become the body of Christ. So we are what we eat. Just as the one bread is baked from many grains and the one wine is pressed from many grapes.

The eucharist is both a sacrifice and banquet in which the mystical body of Christ is offered by Christ, mediator, priest and sacrifice.

Augustine warns us not to stop at the external signs, but rather to go for the deeper spiritual meaning of the eucharist which we eat with our hearts. By partaking of the body and blood of Christ, we participate in eternal life in which we will never hunger or thirst.

Augustine taught a threefold penance. Besides the all-forgiving baptism, daily prayer and charity wipe out minor offenses, while greater sins must be submitted to the Church for public penance. Though Augustine recognized human sinfulness, he also stressed the mercy of God. Yet, we, on our part, have to show a spirit of contrition, penance and forgiveness.

Prayer

Augustine is a man of prayer, influenced by the Neoplatonic ascent to God. And his deep contemplation fired his zeal for souls. Moreover, much of his spiritual counseling consisted in advice on prayer, in particular the Judaeo-Christian *shibboleth* of the Our Father. Not only was Augustine a guide to his flock in Hippo, but also to many sons and daughters in the Lord in distant places. Truly he was a contemplative in action. And though he would have preferred a quiet life of meditative prayer, his episcopal duties took up most of his time.

Hope

Augustine's theology of hope is firmly grounded in sacred scriptures. Hope in the faithful Yahweh rather than his weak creatures is the main theme of the Old Testament, whereas hope in the risen Christ underpins the New. As Paul tells us, the object of hope is an unseen future good. But it must be inspired by love, which gives hope, its drive for the invisible joys of eternal life, or paradise, created by God and restored by the death and resurrection of his divine Son.

Two Cities

In his *The City of God* Augustine answers the accusation of the Romans that Christianity has undermined the Empire by the heretical barbarian invasions from without and their otherworldly asceticism from within. Augustine counters by showing them that there was corruption and injustice in Rome long before the Christians came on the scene.

Furthermore, he develops his theology of the two cities based on the two loves, human and divine. The two cities have their own laws, justice and peace. While the city of man has temporal goals of honor, glory, dominion and wealth, the city of God aims at eternal love, law, justice and peace.

Here on earth the two cities are mixed and in a state of war. But after the last judgment they will be separated. Moreover, those who belong to the city of God should use creatures to help them reach and enjoy eternal life rather than delighting selfishly in earthly pleasures along the way.

Finis

We have seen Augustine's views on some major topics. He has much to say to us today. However, we should read him against his fifth century Christian Roman background. But what makes him a classical author is his ability to narrate his personal beliefs in a way that mirrors those of many of us through the ages. For example, the problem of evil, a doubting faith, youthful loves and marriage, religious vocation, education, a balanced view of this world's successes and failures and finally, a sound theology of God, Christ, Mary, the Church and sacraments, prayer and hope for eternal life.

Augustine's influence on the evolution of Western thought is monumental. His well preserved writings provided a fundamental canon of European theology and philosophy through many different interpretations right up to modern times.

Augustine played a major role in the development of medieval scholasticism from Anselm and Abelard to Peter Damian and Bernard of Clairvaux. Thomas Aquinas incorporated Augustine along with Aristotle and many others into his synthesis. Maritain comments,[1] "Thomas alone was able to extract from Augustine (but with Aristotle's weapons) a science of theology and a science of Christian philosophy." Aquinas favored Aristotle's efficient causality over Augustine's participation.[2] The Franciscans and Augustinians were the main spokesmen of Augustine in the Middle Ages.

During the Renaissance Protestant reformers and Roman Catholics disputed over Augustine's views on justification. And in the seventeenth century

---

1. See J. Maritain, "St. Augustine and St. Thomas Aquinas," in *St. Augustine* (New York: Meridian, 1960), 213.
2. Maritain, "St. Augustine and St. Thomas Aquinas," 218.

there was a revival of Augustinianism among French thinkers including De Berrulle, Montaigne, Descartes and others. Jansenius, De Bay and De Molina held different views on predestination.

Przywara[1] sees modern philosophy beginning with Descartes as a "progressive working out of the Protestant interiority until it becomes the interiority of 'pure intellect,' from the Cartesian 'cogito' to Kant's 'synthetic unity of the ego,' and on to Hegel's 'self-conscious intellect,' a working out of the inner logic of that interiority."

Descartes influenced Spinoza and Malebranche with God assisting our knowing by producing in us our ideas and sensations. Przywara adds, "Augustine, represented by Descartes, achieves his most complete expression in Hegel."[2]

The other Augustine of Pascal is completed in Kierkegaard. This is the romantic Augustine totally submitted to God. Hegel's Augustine is childlike, while Kierkegaard's Augustine is the scandal of the flesh over against the divine majesty. Hegel's Augustianism is dominated by Spinoza's chaste disinterested love of God, which chastity overcomes the paradox of the fear of God in Kierkegaard's Augustinianism.[3]

More recent giants such as Newman and Rahner have built on and corrected Augustine. Like Augustine, Rahner feels compelled to speak on the mysteries even though his language is necessarily unclear.[4] As love is the key to Augustine's thought, so also in Rahner. McCool comments:[5]

> Rahner's theology of charity has combined the phenomenological ontology of Heidegger's authentic human subject, who lets the world of being manifest itself through his authentic self-choice, with the metaphysics of love which Rahner inherited from Augustine and Bonaventure.

As Augustine synthesized Christian tradition with the popular Neoplatonism of his time, so moderns continue to syncretize Christian thought with its gospel, Pauline and Augustinian roots with newer philosophies until we reach the final vision of truth of which our earthly knowledge is but a cloudy reflection.

---

1. E. Przywara, "St. Augustine and the Modern World," in *St. Augustine* (New York: Meridian, 1960), 249-86.

2. Przywara, "St. Augustine and the Modern World," 273-74.

3. Przywara, "St. Augustine and the Modern World," 277.

4. See *Karl Rahner in Dialogue*, P. Imhof and H. Biallowons, eds. (New York: Crossroads), 315.

5. See *A Rahner Reader,* G. McCool, ed. (New York: Seabury, 1975), 239-41.

ABBREVIATIONS

A   *Ancient Christian Writers,* J. Quasten et al., eds., New York, Paulist/Newman

F   *Fathers of the Church,* R. Deferrari, ed., Washington, Catholic University Press

L   Letters

LC   *Loeb Classical Library,* Cambridge, Harvard University Press

N   *A Select Library of the Nicene and Post-Nicene Fathers,* Second Series, P. Schaff and H. Wade, eds., Grand Rapids, Eerdmans

P   *Patrologiae Cursus Completus,* J.-P. Migne, ed., Paris

S   Sermons

SC   *Sources Chrétiennes,* H. DeLubac and J. Daniélou, eds., Paris, Cerf

W   *Works of Saint Augustine, A Translation for the 21st Century,* J. Rotelle, ed., New York, New City Press

A SELECTED BIBLIOGRAPHY

Augustine's Works

The Works of Saint Augustine—A Translation for the 21st Century, New York, New City Press, 1989-.

Patrologia Latina, Paris, Migne, 1844-64.

Corpus Christianorum Ecclesiasticorum Latinorum, Vienna, 1866-.

Corpus Christianorum, Series Latina, Turnai, Brepols, 1955-.

Oeuvres, Bibliothéque Augustinnienne, Paris, Desclée de Brouwer, 1949-.

Biblioteca de Autores Cristianos, Madrid, La Editorial Católica, 1944-.

Sources Chrétiennes, Paris, Cerf, 1960-.

Ancient Christian Writers, Westminster, Newman, 1944-.

A Select Library of the Nicene and Post-Nicene Fathers of the Christian Church, Buffalo, Schaff, 1886-1888.

Fathers of the Church, Washington, Catholic University Press, 1960-.

Some Books on Augustine

Bardy, G., *Saint Augustin,* Paris, Desclée de Brouwer, 1948.

Batterhouse, R., et al., *A Companion to the Study of St. Augustine,* Oxford U. Press, 1955.

Bourke, V., *Augustine's Quest of Wisdom,* Milwaukee, Bruce, 1945.

————., *The Essential Augustine,* New York, Mentor-Omega, 1964.

Brown, P., *Augustine of Hippo,* Berkeley, University of California Press, 1967.

————., *Religion and Society in the Age of Saint Augustine,* New York, Harper and Row, 1972.

Chadwick, H., *Augustine,* New York, Oxford University Press, 1986.

D'Arcy, M., et al., *St. Augustine,* Cleveland, World, 1960.

Fortman, E., *The Triune God,* A Historical Study of the Trinity, Grand Rapids, Baker, 1982.

Gilson, E., *The Christian Philosophy of St. Augustine,* New York, Random House, 1960.

Grabowski, S., *The All Present God, A Study of St. Augustine,* St. Louis, Herder, 1953.

————., *The Church, An Introduction to the Study of St. Augustine,* St. Louis, Herder, 1957.

Hawkins, A. H., *Archetypes of Conversion: Autobiographies of Augustine,* Bunyan and Merton, Lewisburg, Bucknell University Press, 1985.

Markus, R. A., *Saeculum, History and Society in the Theology of Saint Augustine,* Cambridge University Press, 1970.

Marrou, H., *St. Augustine and His Influence Through the Ages,* New York, Harper and Row, 1957.

Marshall, M., *The Restless Heart, The Life and Influence of St. Augustine,* Grand Rapids, Eerdmans, 1987.

Meer, F. van der, *Augustine, the Bishop, The Life and Work of a Father of the Church,* New York, Sheed and Ward, 1961.

Mohler, J., *Late Have I Loved You, An Interpretation of Saint Augustine on Human and Divine Relationships,* New York, New City Press, 1990.

Mourant, H., *An Introduction to the Philosophy of St. Augustine, Selected Readings and Commentaries,* University Park, Pennsylvania University Press, 1964.

Nash, R., *The Light of the Mind, St. Augustine's Theory of Knowledge,* Lexington, University Press of Kentucky, 1969.

Oates, W., *Basic Writings of St. Augustine,* New York, Random House, 1964.

O'Daly, G. J., *Augustine's Philosophy of Mind,* Berkeley, University of California Press, 1987.

O'Donnell, J. J., *Augustine,* Boston, Twayne, 1985.

O'Meara, J., *The Young Augustine: The Growth of St. Augustine's Mind up to His Conversion,* Toronto, Longmans, 1954.

O'Toole, C., *The Philosophy of Creation in the Writings of St. Augustine,* Washington, Catholic University Press, 1944.

Pelikan, J., *The Mystery of Continuity: Time and History, Memory and Eternity in the Thought of St. Augustine,* Charlottesville, University Press of Virginia, 1986.

Pellegrino, M., *The True Priest: The Priesthood as Preached and Practiced by St. Augustine,* Villanova, Augustinian Press, 1988.

Pope, H., *The Teaching of St. Augustine on Prayer and the Contemplative Life,* London, Burns, Oates and Washbourne, 1935.

————., *St. Augustine of Hippo,* Garden City, Doubleday, 1961.

Portaglié, E., *A Guide to the Thought of St. Augustine,* Chicago, Regnery, 1960.

Pryzwara, E., *An Augustine Synthesis,* New York, Harper and Row, 1958.

Rotelle, J., ed., *Augustine Day by Day,* Villanova, Augustinian Press.

Te Selle, E., *Augustine, the Theologian,* New York, Herder and Herder, 1970.

Trapé, A., ed., *My Mother, by Saint Augustine of Hippo,* Villanova, Augustinian Press.

Ulanov, B., *Prayers of Saint Augustine,* Villanova, Augustinian Press.

Wolfson, H., *The Philosophy of the Church Fathers,* Cambridge, Harvard University Press, 1956.

Zumkeller, A., *Augustine's Rule,* Villanova, Augustinian Press.

————., *Augustine's Ideal of the Religious Life,* Villanova, Augustinian Press.

INDEX